ELIM.
Sunday school
Scarborough.

PRESENTED TO

Julie Rogers.

Ist class prize

J. Miller
supt.

J.H.P. Upton
minister

THE DRESDEN SHEPHERDESS

CHRISTINE COURTNEY

LONDON
PICKERING & INGLIS LTD.

PICKERING & INGLIS LTD.
29 Ludgate Hill, London, E.C.4
26 Bothwell Street, Glasgow, C.2

SBN 7208 2065 0

First Published . . . 1960
Reprinted . . . 1969

Printed in Great Britain by
Lowe & Brydone (Printers) Ltd., London

CONTENTS

CHAPTER I

IN THE SAME BOAT

"IT'S a terrible feeling to be left behind." Gillian Dacre watched the big coach until it disappeared down the drive. In it were her fellow-pupils at Deepdene School, hurrying to Swinton Junction to catch their various trains for home, and the glorious freedom of the Easter holidays.

Susan Maitland, standing beside Gillian on the steps of the big grey house, flicked her long fair plait impatiently.

"No need to look like a tragedy queen, Jill. We shall manage to enjoy ourselves somehow."

Gillian's sensitive face flushed at the crisp words and her dark eyes flashed resentfully. It wasn't so bad for Susan. She hadn't missed a lovely holiday with her father in a Lakeland farmhouse. She swallowed the bitter words that were forming as swift compunction seized her. Susan's father was a civil engineer whose contracts frequently took him abroad. His wife usually went with him, so that Susan, having no very near relatives in England, often found herself spending holidays at school.

Gillian gave Susan's arm a repentant squeeze.

"I am glad you're here, Sue. I mean—I'm sorry you can't have a real holiday, but I'm glad we shall be company for each other."

"That's all right." The crisp words rather downed Gillian's sudden enthusiasm, but she was not to know that Susan was determined not to wax sentimental.

That was the road to nowhere. With her laughing blue eyes and roguish dimple she took life as it came, and extracted the utmost enjoyment out of every passing day. She looked at Gillian's sober face and then smiled.

"Let's go and sit on the terrace and make plans. Miss Francis won't be back until supper time. Pity she is staying at school with us, instead of our own Form Mistress."

The April sunshine lay warm on the terrace as the two girls seated themselves outside the open window of the headmistress's sitting-room. Miss Castleton would not have them under her watchful eye, however, for she was already on her way to a well-earned holiday in Italy.

"We definitely must make plans," repeated Susan firmly, as they made themselves comfortable. "There are lots of places we haven't explored yet. Isn't it a blessing Deepdene is where it is, Jill? It might be in some awful smoky town."

Deepdene School was certainly fortunately placed. Situated on the outskirts of the small country town of Duncombe it was surrounded by fields and woods, farms, and deep twisting lanes. Villages and hamlets were tucked away among the hills which rose to a wide expanse of open moorland.

Gillian refused to be wholly consoled. Indeed she was in one of those moods which come to us all at some time. She wanted to find fault with something, or someone.

"I don't believe that Miss Francis will let us go about alone," she responded gloomily. "If we were her own Sixth Formers there might be some hope, but she will think fourteen-year-old Fourth Formers are not to be trusted. It won't be much fun having a mistress tacked on to us all the time."

Susan looked at her companion as though she longed to shake her.

"Gillian Dacre," she exploded, "you are the champion wet blanket. Surely there will be ways and means of getting round Miss Francis. Anyway, let's be constructive for a change. I have a large-scale map and a bus time-table, so we may as well decide where we'd like to go. I'll get them, now." She danced along the terrace and disappeared inside the house.

Left alone Gillian gazed dreamily at the trees and bushes which bordered the long drive to the gate, trying not to think where she might have been had not urgent business robbed Dad and herself of their holiday. Through screening rhododendrons she caught sight of the postman's uniform. He was walking awkwardly, as though his lame leg hurt more than usual.

"I'll run and meet him," thought Gillian, and darted along the terrace and down the steps. "He may have a letter from Dad, and it will save him coming all the way to the house."

She returned in a few minutes carrying two letters for Miss Francis, one for Lucy, the housemaid, and a parcel, which felt like a book, for Susan. No letter from Dad, after all.

Susan was once more seated on the terrace, so Gillian called to her, "A parcel for you, Sue. Catch!"

Gillian's aim was straight but a little too high. Susan jumped and missed. The parcel sailed over her head, and in at the open window of Miss Castleton's sitting-room. There followed a dull thud, accompanied by the sickening sound of breaking china. Gillian's dark eyes met Susan's blue ones in horrified dismay. They stood petrified for several seconds then crept together to the window to inspect the damage.

Susan's parcel lay solidly on the floor, surrounded by what looked like a hundred fragments of china.

"Help!" breathed Gillian, in an appalled voice. "It's Miss Castleton's Dresden Shepherdess."

"*Was*, you mean," Sue corrected her. "It would take a clever china riveter to make that into a Shepherdess again." She was as appalled by the disaster as Gillian, but could not suppress a giggle. "Poor Shepherdess! The parcel scored a direct hit, and knocked her off the bureau into smithereens. What on earth will Miss Castleton say?"

"We shall have to hear what Miss Francis says first," moaned stricken Gillian.

"Why tell her?" suggested Susan quickly. "Don't you see that now we've started off the holiday by smashing Miss Castleton's Shepherdess, Miss Francis is hardly likely to let us go about alone. If she does miss the Shepherdess she will just think Miss Castleton has put it away for safety."

"I jolly well wish she had," lamented Gillian. "The holiday's spoiled now, well and truly. The thought of telling Miss Castleton about this will haunt me waking and sleeping."

"Nonsense," declared Susan optimistically. "We've got to forget it for three weeks." Then sudden inspiration seized her. "I say, Jill. Why shouldn't we try to replace the wretched thing? It will be easier to tell Miss Castleton about the accident knowing we have a substitute Shepherdess to replace it. There are two or three antique shops in Duncombe. If they can't produce a Dresden Shepherdess they'll probably be able to get us one before Miss Castleton returns."

A faint ray of hope lightened the gloom of Gillian's expression.

"China figures will be horribly expensive," she pointed out.

"We can pool our resources. I've got a pound note, as well as three weeks' pocket money. What are you worth?"

"Thirty-two shillings, but I suppose we shall need a bit to spend, and in any case there's no reason why you should contribute, Sue. I broke the wretched thing by throwing that parcel. It's up to me to shoulder all the blame."

"Rubbish!" scoffed Susan. "I missed the catch. We're both in the same boat, and we ride out the storm together," she said grandly. "But first we must make love to Lucy for a brush and dustpan on some pretext and remove all traces of our crime."

CHAPTER II

A TRIAL TRIP

THAT evening when Susan and Gillian presented themselves in the Junior Common Room for supper, Miss Francis was already seated at the table. She greeted them pleasantly.

"I hope you've had a nice day. Now we are together we must talk over arrangements for the holidays. Miss Hunter has agreed to continue your riding lessons seeing you have to remain at school, and she is expecting you at ten o'clock to-morrow morning. On Friday I thought we could visit Waterstone Castle, and on Saturday perhaps take a picnic lunch to Rocombe and collect primroses and daffodils to decorate the church for Easter Day." Miss Francis smiled across at them. "Really, there are so many lovely places to visit, there'll be some happy jaunts in store for us."

Susan and Gillian agreed politely, but with a marked lack of enthusiasm which evidently Miss Francis observed for there was a spark of indignation in her grey eyes and an edge of sharpness to her voice as she continued:

"I've also arranged for you two girls to sleep together in the Primrose Room. I can see that idea appeals to you."

The glum faces opposite her brightened at once.

The idea of sleeping in the Primrose Room certainly did appeal to Susan and Gillian. Usually this was the room shared by the School Captain and Games Captain. It was the most desirable room in the house. Situated at the end of a corridor occupied by mistresses and seniors it was some distance from the main staircase and possessed, in addition to its other attractions, its own special fire escape.

"We should love to sleep in the Primrose Room, Miss Francis," enthused Gillian, and Susan added, "Can we move in to-night, please?"

"Yes, you may take your things there directly after supper, but come down again for prayers before you go to bed."

She broke the silence that followed by a timely reminder that she was not there for the sole benefit of two fourth formers. "By the way," she said, "I am spending the holidays at school in order to complete some special private work and my time is rather precious. I trust you will both realise that."

The rebuke brought a flush to Gillian's cheeks, but Susan did not seem unduly impressed.

It was fun taking possession of the pretty room with its twin divans, curtains and covers gay with bunches of primroses, and especially nice furniture.

Susan wasted no time in exploring. She tried the bolts of the door leading to the fire escape, and was delighted to discover that they were well-oiled and slid back noiselessly. The dimple dipped mischievously in her cheek.

"We may find this way out useful, Jill. I foresee Miss Francis is going to be a bit sticky about expeditions on our own. But seeing her time is rather precious she needn't bother to waste it on us."

Gillian nodded gloomily.

"If she becomes too conscientious about us I can't

see much chance of looking round the antique shops for a Dresden Shepherdess."

"Oh, we'll find a way," said Susan, with characteristic optimism. "Anyhow, it was decent of Miss Francis to put us in here, but fancy wanting us down again for prayers! I think she might have let us off in the holidays. We can say our prayers up here just as well."

Gillian mumbled something non-committal as they closed the door of the Primrose Room and went downstairs. For herself she liked the morning and evening prayers which were an institution at Deepdene School. It was inspiring to gather in the Assembly Hall and hear Miss Castleton read a passage from the Bible in her clear, beautifully modulated voice. She enjoyed singing the hymns, too, and joining reverently in the prayers they all repeated together.

Miss Francis read some verses from the tenth chapter of John, and as Gillian listened to the words, "My sheep hear My voice and I know them and they follow Me: and I give unto them eternal life and they shall never perish, neither shall any man pluck them out of My hand," she thought that even spoken in Miss Francis' rather prosy voice, they sounded like a lovely poem.

Back upstairs again the two girls quickly prepared for bed, and were soon snuggling down luxuriously in the twin divans. As Gillian lay drowsily awaiting sleep the words she had just heard floated through her mind, My sheep hear My voice and I know them and they follow Me.

"I'd like to know I was one of them," she thought rather wistfully. "I wonder how one can be sure. I'll—"

Susan bounced up suddenly in the other bed.

"Jill! I've just thought of something. My parcel is still in Miss Castleton's sitting-room. I remember kicking it under the bureau when we were cleaning up the wreck of the Shepherdess."

"Oh well it won't hurt until morning," said Gillian cosily.

"All the same, I'm going down to get it."

The next moment Susan had swung her feet out of bed and reached for her dressing-gown.

Startled by her sudden action Gillian sat up and said earnestly:

"Sue, you mustn't. If you did happen to run into Miss Francis she'll give us separate bedrooms. Don't go, Sue."

"Now, Jill, don't panic," advised the irrepressible Susan. "Miss Francis will be safe in her den busy on that special work of hers. The side door is always unlocked until cook and Lucy go to bed, and I can find my way blindfold from the side door to Miss Castleton's sitting-room. I'll be back with that parcel before you can say Jack Robinson."

Susan softly drew back the bolts of the fire escape door and stepped out on to the platform.

With misgiving, Gillian watched her run lightly down the iron staircase, and disappear into the house through the side door. Then she returned to bed to await, with growing alarm, her friend's return.

Meanwhile, Susan had reached Miss Castleton's sitting-room safely, and was groping round it bumping herself against the furniture, for she dared not switch on a light. At last she located the bureau and had just succeeded in retrieving her parcel when a pencil of yellow light appeared beneath the door. Then she heard the sound of the door handle being turned. Somebody was coming into the room.

Right beside her hung one of the heavy blue velvet curtains which Miss Castleton liked to draw across the bay window on winter evenings. Still kneeling, Susan edged behind it, congratulating herself that her dressing-gown was almost the same colour as the curtain. Even if she was not completely hidden, and the intruder switched on a light, she would not be too conspicuous.

With fast beating heart Susan watched Miss Francis come into the room. She carried a torch. Crossing to the book-shelves she directed its beam along the rows of books until she found the one she wanted. Then to Susan's intense dismay she sat down with it at Miss Castleton's desk, and switched on the small shaded desk light. For ten long minutes Susan knelt in an agony of suspense while the Mistress made notes on a scribbling pad. Then she realised with horror that she was going to sneeze. Desperately she pinched her nose and pressed hard on her upper lip. The spasm passed, but it left her shaken, and she dreaded a return of the fatal tickle in her nostrils.

At long last Miss Francis rose, replaced the book, picked up her torch and, hugging her scribbling pad, walked quickly out of the room.

Susan gave her sufficient time to get well away, then she groped her way out into the hall, and slipped silent as a shadow along the passage to the side door. As she sped up the fire staircase she heard the key turn in the lock.

"Just made it," she breathed.

Gillian hardly waited for her to enter the room before she began:

"Sue, I've been terribly worried. Whatever—"

She broke off in alarm as footsteps approached along the corridor. Susan flung herself into bed and drew the bedclothes up to her chin. The door opened, and Miss Francis surveyed the room by the light of her carefully shaded torch. Satisfied that all was well she closed the door gently, and went off to enjoy a luxurious hour reading in bed.

"Sue," began Gillian again after a safe interval, "I've been terribly worried. Whatever happened?"

"Just a minute, and I'll tell you."

Susan crept to the fire escape door and noiselessly slid the bolts across.

"It was a near thing, Jill, but I've got my parcel and I've tested our escape route. I have more than a faint idea we are going to find that very useful. Very useful, indeed!"

CHAPTER III

GILLIAN GOES ALONE

GILLIAN awoke early next morning and lay for a while wondering why a weight of depression rested on her spirit. Then she remembered the broken Shepherdess. The events of the previous day, culminating with Susan's daring trip to Miss Castleton's sitting-room, floated across her mind. She seemed to hear again her friend saying, 'I've tested our escape route. I have more than a faint idea we are going to find that useful. Very useful indeed.'

The echo of the words gave her an idea. She turned over and consulted the wrist-watch on her bedside table. It was barely a quarter to seven. Suddenly Gillian felt it would be impossible to lie there just thinking about the broken Shepherdess. She must *do* something. A glance at the other divan showed her that Susan was still sweetly sleeping; her fair plait hanging over the edge of the divan, a smile hovering round her lips.

"It looks as though she's having pleasant dreams," thought Gillian a trifle resentfully. "I won't wake her, but I've a good mind to run into Duncombe, and have a peep in the nearest antique shop, just to see if there is any sign of Dresden china. I can slip down the fire escape and be back long before breakfast."

She slid out from between the sheets, seized her clothes and tiptoed to the bathroom.

'What about the strict rule that no girl must visit

Duncombe without permission', nagged her conscience, 'and never in any circumstances alone'?

"Rules don't apply in holiday time," Gillian quietened the disturbing thought. "Anyway, if Sue is awake when I go back to the Primrose Room, I'll get her to come with me."

When Gillian crept back, however, Susan was still fast asleep, so after a moment's indecision Jill crossed to the fire escape door, opened it noiselessly, stepped outside, and closed it gently behind her. Lightly she sped down the iron staircase.

She knew that cook and Lucy would be up by this time, but she calculated that their duties would keep them occupied on the other side of the house. If she ran through the kitchen garden, skirted the tennis courts, and crossed the playing field to a lane on the far side, she would be safe from observation. The lane would bring her out into the Duncombe road quite a bit nearer to the town.

She hurried along, too intent on her errand to appreciate the beauty of the early April morning. Her goal was an antique shop in Bell Street, a turning off the busy High Street.

Reaching the shop without mishap Gillian prepared to make a careful study of its two windows. These were so crammed with a conglomeration of objects of all kinds that it took some time to master their contents. A prolonged scrutiny at length convinced Gillian that the windows contained few china pieces, and certainly nothing remotely resembling Miss Castleton's Dresden Shepherdess.

Disappointed, she retraced her steps to the High Street. She turned the corner, and received a nasty shock. Not many yards away, Miss Ross, the visiting mistress who taught drawing and handicrafts at Deepdene, was waiting for the bus. She carried sketching paraphernalia, and was evidently going off early to catch the morning light for a picture. Fortunately for Gillian Miss Ross happened to be facing the other way, so she was able to dodge back into Bell Street without being seen.

"Bother!" she exclaimed. "I shall have to go to the top of Bell Street and turn right, and hope I can turn right again, and come out into the road beyond the end of High Street."

A turning to the right at the top of Bell Street brought her to a lane which ran right and left. Relieved, she started to walk to the right down the lane.

At a little distance along it road works were in progress. A quantity of equipment, half a dozen red lamps, extinguished now as it was broad daylight, and a watchman's hut were at one side of the lane. On the other side a steep grass bank rose to a hedge-enclosed field in which a flock of sheep were grazing. A weed-grown ditch separated the foot of the bank from the ashphalted lane.

Suddenly the air was filled with agitated 'baa-ing.' As Gillian watched, startled, the sheep responsible for the outcry scrambled up the grass bank and squeezed through a gap in the hedge. Beside the ditch an old man drew himself slowly upright, and turned at the sound of Gillian's approaching footsteps. He jerked his head in the direction of the vanished sheep.

"'Tis a mercy for her I happened to be by," he told Gillian, "otherwise the poor thing might've struggled in that ditch for a long time. When a ewe slips and lands on her back 'tis uncommon difficult for her to rise again without aid."

"Is it?" asked Gillian, gazing interestedly at this watchman, who looked so unusually spic and span. His blue eyes twinkled back at her in friendly fashion.

"'Tis indeed. The weight of their wool makes it a job for them to regain their equilibrium." The old man pronounced the word with great deliberation and went on, "Isn't it strange, now, with all that good grass in the field that sheep must break through the hedge thinking 'tis juicier on the bank outside? There, we can't afford to judge them, for we're as bad ourselves. The Bible says so. All we like sheep have gone astray; we have turned every one to his own way, and the Lord hath laid on Him the iniquity of us all. Aye the Good Shepherd gave His life for the sheep."

Gillian was much too interested in this surprising conversation to think what Miss Francis's reaction might be could she see her at the present moment.

"That came in our reading last night," she said eagerly.

"Did it now? A wonderful chapter the tenth of John. It shows us up for what we are, witless wandering sheep, sadly in need of the Good Shepherd who loved us enough to die instead of us, and wants to lead us all our lives. We're not really safe till we can say, like David, 'the Lord is *my* shepherd.' " Then suddenly the corners of the old watchman's eyes crinkled in a smile, and he said as though astonished at himself: "Here am I preaching a sermon instead of getting my breakfast. Can I offer you a cup of tea, my dear?"

Gillian had been about to ask a question or two, but the word 'breakfast' affected her like a mild electric shock.

"No, thank you, I'm going to be frightfully late if I

don't rush madly. Good-bye," and she fled along the lane.

Hot and breathless she toiled up the steps of the fire escape, opened the door of the Primrose Room, and met the hostile blue gaze of an indignant Susan.

"I was just going down without you," she told Gillian distantly. "I call it jolly mean, to trail off somewhere on your own. You'd better do something to your hair before Miss Francis sees you. I don't know what you've been up to, but you look as though you've come through a hedge backwards."

While Gillian hastily tidied her hair, she endeavoured to placate her friend. "You were fast asleep, Sue. I didn't like to wake you. I only went to Duncombe to look in the nearest antique shop, just to see whether there was a Dresden Shepherdess. There wasn't," she added despondently.

Susan listened to her explanation in stony silence, and stalked ahead of her downstairs. However, it was not in Sue's nature to cherish resentment for very long, especially on a fine April morning, and with a riding lesson in prospect. At a turn of the stair she caught sight of Gillian's miserable face and compunction seized her. She waited for her friend to catch up, and gave her arm a forgiving squeeze.

"Don't worry, Jill," she consoled. "You've only looked in *one* antique shop. I'm sure there are at least two others, and we'll find an opportunity to look in them at the earliest possible moment."

Gillian smiled gratefully, returning Sue's squeeze, and peace restored between them, they joined an impatiently-waiting Miss Francis at the breakfast table.

CHAPTER IV

SUSAN MAKES AN ENEMY

AS they walked down the drive a short time later to catch the bus which would take them to Rockleigh for their riding lesson, Gillian was tempted to tell Susan about her meeting with the old watchman. She longed to pass on the information that the weight of wool carried by sheep made it difficult for them to regain their feet if they fell, and she wanted to know what Sue thought of the old man's talk about the Good Shepherd.

Once or twice she almost started to speak, but she felt it would not be tactful to enlarge on the morning's expedition. So she pushed the subject to the back of her mind, resolving to take Susan to visit the watchman should they manage to get into Duncombe on their own in a further search for a Dresden Shepherdess.

"Do come on, Jill," an impatient voice broke in on her thoughts. We're going to miss the bus and our riding lesson if you don't hurry."

They just managed to catch the bus which took them to Rockleigh post office. Here, they alighted and turned down the lane beside the forge which led to Rockleigh Riding School.

The riding school was owned and run by two ex-pupils of 'Deepdene', Pamela and Julie Hunter. They were both qualified riding instructresses and accomplished horsewomen.

When Susan and Gillian pushed open the door of the

stableyard they found that Miss Pamela Hunter and her sister were in the paddock taking jumping practice with some earlier comers. Brian Timms, the young groom, was cleaning tack in the harness room.

"Hullo!" he called, "going to show us how to jump this morning?"

Neither of the girls liked his familiar tone and impudent look. Susan tossed her head without replying, and stalked across the yard to greet Puck, her favourite pony. She was a good rider, possessing confidence, perfect balance and complete control of her mount. Jumping was her especial joy. Gillian, for her part, disliked jumping, and would only ride Silverspot, a gentle amiable little creature, the ideal pony for a riding school. He caught sight of her now and whinneyed in anticipation of the lump of sugar she never forgot to bring for him. Gillian walked towards him, followed by Susan, who had decided to watch the jumping in the paddock. Patch, Miss Hunter's fox-terrier puppy, ran in front of the two girls into the harness room.

Susan, a few yards behind Gillian, reached the door of the harness room in time to see Brian Timms lift Patch with his foot and send him hurtling under a bench. Yelping with fright the puppy rolled over and over. Susan's blue eyes flashed as she said scornfully:

"You coward."

She picked up frightened, whimpering Patch and soothed him with endearing words and caresses.

Brian Timms scowled at her muttering, "Silly, stuck-up school kid, making a fuss about a dog that isn't hurt, anyway."

Susan satisfied herself that Patch was not really injured and put him down. He made a quick exit from the harness room and Susan turned to follow him, but as she passed Brian Timms he stuck out a foot. Susan tripped over it and fell headlong, narrowly missing a puddle left by a recent shower: her humiliation was heightened by Brian Timms' guffaw.

Fortunately Miss Hunter had witnessed the stable-lad's treatment of both Patch and Susan, for she had been looking through the back window of the harness room.

Her lips tightened. This confirmed an opinion which had been hardening for some time that Timms was not suitable for riding-school work. On Saturday she would give him a fortnight's wages in lieu of notice and send him packing.

When Miss Hunter came round to the front of the harness room, Susan was just getting to her feet. "I slipped," she explained to the mistress. "But I'm not hurt."

Miss Hunter and her sister Julie, strikingly alike with hazel eyes, brown hair, and outdoor-looking complexions, soon had Susan and Gillian busy at the jumps in the paddock. After jumping was over they took them into their bungalow for coffee before setting out on a ride together.

The two Miss Hunters were still young enough to be interested in school affairs, and it wasn't very long before Susan confided to them the tragic fate of the Dresden Shepherdess.

"Golly!" exclaimed Julie, with more force than elegance, "d'you mean to say you've actually smashed the thing?"

"To smithereens," confirmed Susan.

"Well, I'm not going to pretend I'm sorry," said Pamela Hunter smiling. "Whenever I was on the carpet in Miss Castleton's study I felt that wretched Shepherdess was eyeing me with smug superiority. Her fate leaves me unmoved."

"We're going to try and replace the Shepherdess," put in Susan quickly, "if we can dodge Miss Francis long enough to poke round the antique shops."

Julie Hunter looked thoughtful. "Ever since you mentioned the Shepherdess I've been trying to remember where I'd seen another one—but I don't think it was in a shop." She appealed to her sister. "You remember when we bought Silverspot from Mrs. Perry we went into her parlour, as she called it? I'm sure she had a Dresden Shepherdess on a corner bracket."

"Can't say I noticed it," shrugged Pamela Hunter, "and even if she had one, Julie, she might not want to sell it."

"But there would be no harm in asking," said Susan, hopefully. She produced a pencil and battered diary from her pocket, and asked for the address of Mrs. Perry. With glee she wrote it: Mrs. Perry, Twin Gables, Rocombe.

Riding back to school in the bus later on she and Gillian congratulated themselves on their good fortune.

"To think," said Susan jubilantly, "that Mrs. Perry, who owns a Shepherdess, actually lives at Rocombe, and we're going there on Saturday to gather primroses and daffodils."

Gillian was more cautious in her satisfaction.

"Don't forget that Miss Francis will be with us, and we may not be able to call on Mrs. Perry."

Susan refused to be daunted.

"We'll find a way all right, when the time comes."

CHAPTER V

A DISASTROUS EXPEDITION

WHEN Susan and Gillian arrived back at school, one o'clock dinner was waiting, and Miss Francis told them curtly to wash their hands and be quick about it.

"A bit scratchy, isn't she?" grimaced Susan as she and Gillian carried out the instruction.

If the two girls had not been so absorbed in their own affairs they might have noticed that Miss Francis looked white and strained, and that she drew in her breath sharply from time to time as though in pain. She made no complaint, however, and spent the afternoon helping the girls to improve their tennis. After tea she retired to her den to put in an hour or two at her 'special' work leaving Susan and Gillian to tackle a mammoth jig-saw puzzle.

Next morning, the weather was unsettled with sunshine and showers alternating, but Miss Francis decreed there was no need to forego the excursion to Waterstone Castle.

"We shall be under cover most of the time," she said, "so we can dodge the showers. There is a good café in Waterstone village which caters for visitors to the castle so we need not bother about taking a picnic lunch. On the way back we can have an early cup of tea in Swinton and be home in good time for supper."

It sounded all right, but as Gillian said to Susan when they were alone, "it doesn't leave much scope for dodging Miss Francis."

When the three of them were travelling in the bus through the lanes towards Swinton, Susan and Gillian were silent, occupied with their thoughts. Susan was turning over in her mind various wild schemes for 'losing' Miss Francis in busy Swinton, and making a quick dash around the shops, while Gillian sat wondering whether she could possibly summon courage to talk to the mistress about the chapter she had read on the first evening of the holidays.

It was a pretty ride past fields and farms with clusters of outbuildings, by woods where primroses gleamed like pale sunshine beneath the trees, and in and out of hamlets whose cottage gardens were gay with daffodils and polyanthus.

At Swinton they changed into a small local bus for the last stage of their journey to Waterstone, a village nestling at the foot of the hill which was crowned by the castle.

Miss Francis called at the café to make sure they could provide a hot lunch about twelve-thirty, then led the way up to the castle gate.

The ancient building was now largely a ruin but there was enough still standing to make it worth a visit. Miss Francis took her charges to the ramparts first to admire the view then conducted them round the castle. She knew its history, and told several stories and legends as she pointed out the beauty of stone carving, graceful arch, or exquisitely designed window.

Susan yawned behind her hand, but Gillian listened entranced. A sharp shower of rain about twelve drove them down to the café a little earlier for lunch than expected.

Susan's boredom vanished at the sight of steak and kidney pie, and Gillian discovered suddenly that she was hungry, too, but Miss Francis ate practically nothing. Even fruit salad and cream failed to tempt her, and she made do with sipping at her coffee.

By the time they had finished lunch the sun was shining again, and Miss Francis suggested walking back to Swinton.

"There is nothing else to see in Waterstone, and we have an hour to wait for the next bus, so we will have a look at the Swinton shops."

Susan grinned when she heard this suggestion, recalling how she had racked her brain to secure just such an opportunity.

The three of them reached Swinton safely and were just about to cross the busy High Street, when without warning Miss Francis collapsed and slumped heavily against Susan. Fortunately sturdy Susan was able to support her so that she fell on the pavement and not in the road. Then she knelt beside the prostrate mistress, remembering that it is necessary to loosen the clothing of a person who has fainted. Gillian knelt too, her dark eyes wide and frightened.

In no time at all a small crowd collected and a policeman appeared on the scene. A nurse, just off duty from the hospital, hurried up to help.

"It isn't just an ordinary fainting fit," she told the policeman. "This lady is very ill, and we should get her to hospital without delay."

The policeman nodded.

"The ambulance is on the way, nurse. Ah! here it comes."

In a very short time Miss Francis had been lifted into the ambulance, and the driver was ready to speed away.

"I'll come with you," said the kindly nurse, smiling

reassuringly at Susan and Gillian. "You will be wanted to give particulars in case the patient isn't able to do so."

White-faced and silent Susan and Gillian sat side by side in the ambulance, Susan holding Miss Francis's umbrella while Gillian feverishly clutched her handbag.

On arrival at the hospital Miss Francis was wheeled away for examination, and Gillian and Susan were told to wait in a pleasant ante-room.

The friendly nurse suggested they should look in Miss Francis's handbag and see whether she had an address book which might give the telephone number or address of her parents. She also told them what other particulars might be required, and then hurried away to her duties.

Presently a white-coated doctor came to tell the waiting girls that Miss Francis was suffering from acute appendicitis, and an immediate operation would be necessary. He asked for the address and telephone number of the patient's nearest relatives, and Gillian, having found an address book was able to supply the required information.

"You could wait here until after the operation if you would like to," the doctor told them. "We shall, of course, notify the patient's parents at once, but they cannot be here just yet."

"Is there anything we can do to help?" quavered Gillian desperately.

"Yes, you can pray," smiled the doctor, "that will be a splendid help." He nodded towards a framed parchment scroll on the wall beside her and went quickly from the room.

Gillian turned and read the words on the scroll.

"'God is our refuge and strength, a very present

help in trouble!' Oh! Sue, we must just pray hard."

After a while Susan grew restless. "I think we ought to let Miss Hunter know about Miss Francis," she whispered. "I'll go and see if I can find a telephone kiosk anywhere."

She went off, and presently returned to say that she had found a telephone box, and had spoken to Miss Hunter.

"The news was an awful shock," she told Gillian, "and Miss Hunter and Miss Julie are coming to Swinton Hospital to collect us as fast as their old car will bring them."

By the time the two Miss Hunters reached the hospital the operation had been successfully performed, though Miss Francis was, of course, still under the anaesthetic, and her condition would be critical for a time.

When the doctor brought this news he smiled encouragingly at Susan and Gillian.

"Keep on praying. I'm sure you must have prayed already. It is a powerful help in times of stress and danger."

Driving home to Deepdene in the old, but still comfortable car the tension of the past hours relaxed a little. Susan's elastic spirits rose with every yard covered, and her cheeks regained their normal pink hue as she told Miss Hunter and her sister the story of the eventful day. Gillian, still looking pale and shaken gazed silently out of the window.

As the car left Duncombe High Street and turned into the road which ran past 'Deepdene' she glanced along the side lane where road works were in progress. She caught a brief glimpse of red lamps and a coke brazier glowing in front of the watchman's hut. Scraps of his conversation about sheep floated across her tired mind. She was brought back to the present by Miss Hunter saying soothingly:

"I've broken the news to cook and Lucy and cook will have a good meal ready to sustain you, after your ordeal, and I should go to bed directly you've eaten it," she advised the girls. "By the way, what are you doing to-morrow?"

"Miss Francis was going to take us to Rocombe to pick primroses and daffodils to decorate the church," said Susan. "We could still do that."

"A good idea," agreed Miss Hunter. "It will be better than sitting at home, moping and worrying."

To the credit of both girls be it said that neither of them gave a thought to the fact that they could now call on Mrs. Perry without hindrance and ask whether she would be willing to sell them her Dresden Shepherdess.

CHAPTER VI

IT'S OURS—FOR FIVE POUNDS

WHEN Susan and Gillian presented themselves belatedly for breakfast next morning, Lucy told them that Miss Pamela Hunter had just 'phoned after telephoning the hospital.

"Miss Francis had a comfortable night, and she is definitely a little better this morning."

Gillian and Susan exchanged pleased smiles, feeling happy that their prayers had helped in the crisis.

"Now you can go off to Rocombe with easy minds," said Lucy benevolently. "Cook has put a picnic lunch in the haversack for you, and you can take this wide, flat basket for your flowers."

It was a lovely April morning, and as the two girls walked down the drive to catch the quarter-past-ten bus their spirits rose higher with every step. Birds were twittering and calling to one another in the trees, and the rhododendron buds were swelling visibly. High white clouds sailed lazily across the blue above them, and the sun was warm on their faces as they turned down Market Street to board the bus.

By eleven o'clock they were standing outside the post office in Rocombe debating whether to gather the daffodils and primroses first, or settle with Mrs. Perry.

Rocombe was divided into three distinct sections, the village street stretching for more than a mile. The post office stood in the middle section. Cleat Lane, where the best primroses grew, turned off the section away to the left, and the daffodil field lay a quarter of a mile beyond the section to the right. The girls had not thought to ask Miss Hunter in which section 'Twin Gables' could be found.

"Let's pick daffodils first," voted Gillian, "because the daffodil field will be the best place for lunch."

"O.K.," agreed Susan, "and we'll keep a look-out as we go along, in case 'Twin Gables' is this way." None of the houses they passed, however, bore this name.

"Just as well, perhaps," dimpled Susan, "we shall feel stronger to tackle Mrs. Perry after lunch."

The daffodil field was separated from the road by a rough stone wall, and sloped gently to a fast flowing river. Hundreds of golden blossoms, smelling faintly sweet, were nodding in the breeze. Quickly Susan and Gillian scrambled over the wall, lined their basket with leaves, then half-filled it with bunches of carefully selected flowers.

"Now for lunch," said Gillian, picking up the haversack. "Let's sit on the wall with our backs to the road. It's warm and sunny there."

Side by side they sat in great contentment munching ham sandwiches and sausage rolls, and looking about them. They now noticed something which they had failed to see whilst busy gathering flowers. A narrow lane ran down at one side of the field and halfway along it stood a solitary house; a white-washed dwelling with a green roof. It had a narrow gable at either end, in each of which was set a round window, looking rather like a surprised eye.

"Somebody is shaking a duster out of one of the windows," remarked Sue. "Evidently they're very house-proud."

"They're shaking it a jolly long time," was Gillian's comment a few minutes later. "It's still waving madly." Her voice rose sharply. "Sue—I think they're signalling or something."

Susan grinned. "They certainly won't be signalling to us."

Gillian looked all around. "They must be, Sue. There's nobody else about, and it wouldn't be much good signalling to cars tearing along this road."

"P'raps we had better investigate, then." Susan jumped down and picked up the basket, while Gillian stuffed the remains of their lunch in the haversack.

They climbed over the wall and set off down the lane. As they approached the cottage, Gillian pointed out the name, 'Twin Gables' in faded lettering on the gate. "Mrs. Perry's house," she whispered nervously.

The window in one of the gables opened wide and a pleasant faced, middle-aged woman looked out.

"I've been signalling to you frantically," she called, "and I was afraid you weren't going to take any notice. I'm locked in, and it's my own fault. One of the knobs has come off the handle of this door. Without thinking I opened the window, the door banged, and the handle fell out on the other side. I didn't have any pliers handy to turn the lock, so here I've been, a prisoner. The back door is unlocked. Do run round, one of you, and come up and let me out."

Susan put down her basket, ran round to the back and upstairs, and in a very few minutes had set the captive free.

"Thank you very much, my dear," beamed a grateful Mrs. Perry. "I'm more than glad to be out of that. I watched you eating your lunch, and it made me hungrier than I was already. I'm going to make some coffee straight away. You must join me. I noticed you had nothing to drink with your lunch."

The joyful barking of a dog startled Susan.

"That's Rufus," smiled his mistress. "He wonders where I've been. It's a mercy I shut him in the kitchen when I went upstairs, or he wouldn't have let you rescue me. Fetch your friend, and I'll introduce you both to him."

Rufus was introduced with due ceremony, and then their hostess told the girls what they already knew, that her name was Mrs. Perry.

"We are Susan Maitland and Gillian Dacre," they introduced themselves in turn.

In a very short time they were sitting in the cheerful kitchen enjoying coffee and biscuits.

Mrs. Perry quickly put them at their ease and they found themselves telling her about the holidays they were spending at school, and Miss Francis's sudden illness. They went on to talk of the two Miss Hunters and Rockleigh Riding School, and when Gillian had pleased Mrs. Perry by warm praise of Silverspot, Susan judged it a good moment to explain about the accident to Miss Castleton's Dresden Shepherdess.

She cleared her throat and then began impulsively.

"Miss Hunter told us that you have a Shepherdess," she finished breathlessly, "a Dresden Shepherdess—and we wondered whether you would be willing to sell it?"

Mrs. Perry looked startled.

"I've never thought of selling my Shepherdess," she said slowly, "though truth to tell I'm in need of ready cash just now, as I shall soon be faced with a big bill for repairs. But you see the Dresden Shepherdess was given to me by my grandmother, and it had belonged to her mother, so it is very old—a sort of family heirloom. Granny always told me to take great care of it."

"Oh!" cried Gillian in quick disappointment, "of course you won't want to part with it if it's so precious."

"Heirlooms are all very well," smiled Mrs. Perry, "but a sound roof over one's head is much more important. It is for repairs to the roof, among other things, that I need the extra money."

She hesitated for a moment, then finally made up her mind.

"You two helped me out of my fix, so I'd like to help you out of yours. How will it do if I let you have my Shepherdess for five pounds? I think that would be a fair price."

Gillian gasped, torn between dismay and joy, but before she could speak Sue cut in, "Thank you, very much, Mrs. Perry. Can you give us a little time to pay? You keep the Shepherdess, of course, until we bring the money."

"Bless you, my dear, there's no desperate hurry. I haven't even had the estimate for the work yet." She sighed, and said sadly, "I was saving up to visit my daughter Sylvia, but the money will have to go another way now. My grandson is nine months old, and I've never seen him and I was so looking forward to a few weeks with them all. That's my grandson's photo on the mantelpiece. Isn't he a lovely boy?"

As they looked at the photograph the girls noticed the clock and saw how the time had flown.

"Sue!" exclaimed Gillian in alarm. "We must go. We've got to walk back to Cleat Lane to pick primroses, and if we miss the three o'clock bus Miss Hunter will start worrying."

"I still own the paddock I used for Silverspot," said Mrs. Perry kindly, "and under the hedges there you'll find finer primroses than any in Cleat Lane. Go and pick as many as you like. It will save you a lot of time."

Their baskets well filled with fragrant bunches, the two girls bid a grateful goodbye to Mrs. Perry and Rufus, and set off for the village and the bus.

"I'm glad Mrs. Perry has Rufus to take care of her," said Gillian, glancing back at the solitary house. After a short silence she burst out, "Sue! what was the use of asking for time to pay for the Shepherdess? How can we possibly raise five pounds?"

"Earn it!" replied Susan tersely. Then she chuckled at Gillian's astounded expression. "There must be dozens of ways of earning money," she urged, "and it's up to us to think of some if we want the Dresden Shepherdess. Think, Jill, think. It's ours—for five pounds, and when we've got it we're trouble free."

CHAPTER VII

THE SHEEP—MY SHEEP

GILLIAN and Susan had thought of no possible way of earning money by the time they arrived back at 'Deepdene', but their own preoccupation was dispelled when they were met in the hall by Lucy, who informed them with an air of great importance, that she had received a telephone call from Miss Francis's parents.

"They're staying at a hotel in Swinton for the week-end," she told the girls, "and they've been to see Miss Francis. She is still very ill, but holding her own, and the improvement is being maintained."

"Good. Thank you, Lucy. We're just going to 'phone Miss Hunter to let her know we are safely back, so we'll pass on the news to her."

Susan raced Gillian to the telephone. Directly after an early tea the two girls took their basket of flowers along to the church and stayed to help in the work of decoration.

Gillian was placing a bowl of their primroses on a window ledge when a voice beside her remarked pleasantly:

"What beautiful primroses! I'm sure I've never seen finer ones."

"They came from a private paddock," explained Gillian, turning to face the speaker.

The lady was a stranger, but Gillian could not have said afterwards whether she was tall or short, dark or fair, for her attention was held by a pair of brown eyes, shining with such friendliness and sincerity that they drew her like a magnet.

"I'm the rector's sister, Eleanor Blain," she introduced herself, "and I'm only here for the weekend. I meant to arrive in time to help decorate but I was delayed, and now things seem well under way, and my services not needed."

"Perhaps you'd like to finish the window ledges with me?" suggested Gillian, indicating other bowls and flowers awaiting attention. "I'm Gillian Dacre," she continued rather shyly, "and Sue and I are spending the holidays at school. That's Sue, helping with the font."

Together Miss Blain and Gillian worked their way down the church towards the magnificent west window. The rays of the setting sun were pouring through it, causing the colours to glow like jewels, and lighting up the face of the Good Shepherd, bent lovingly over the lamb He carried. His look was full of compassion and tenderness; his bearing gentle and gracious.

"What a splendid window," murmured Miss Blain. "A very lovely portrayal of the Good Shepherd. 'My sheep hear My voice and I know them and they follow Me,' " she repeated softly. "How safe we are when we can say, the Lord is *my* Shepherd."

"Oh!" cried Gillian startled, "that's what the old watchman said," She rushed on, in answer to Miss Blain's look of enquiry, "and that verse came in our reading. I was going to ask Miss Francis about it."

"You *were* going to. Does that mean something prevented you? If so, will I do instead?" Gillian hesitated, and Miss Blain continued encouragingly.

"We've finished our flowers. Suppose we sit down in this side pew for a few minutes, and I'll see whether I can help."

Her warm smile was irresistible, and Gillian blurted out confusedly.

"I just wondered—what is the difference between the sheep and my sheep, if there *is* a difference."

"Yes, dear, there is a difference. Perhaps I can explain it this way. The Bible says, All we like sheep have gone astray; we have turned every one to his own way; and the Lord hath laid on Him the iniquity of us *all*. Our sin separated us from God and deserved His just judgment, but in His love He devised a plan whereby we could be forgiven and could return to Him. He gave His Son, the Good Shepherd, and the Good Shepherd gave Himself willingly, to die on Calvary, and bear God's judgment against the sin of the whole world. So you see everyone is included in the sheep for whom the Good Shepherd died.

"If, though, we want to be numbered among those whom the Good Shepherd referred to as 'my sheep', we have to make it a personal matter. We must believe that the Good Shepherd died instead of me; that He paid the penalty for my sin and because He did God can forgive me and accept me in Him.

"If you do that, Gillian, God will forgive you and put His Spirit in your heart, and you will become one of the sheep who hear the Shepherd's voice, and who love Him and follow Him. I hope I've made it clear?"

"Yes, thank you," said Gillian. Out of the corner of her eye she could see Susan signalling to her to hurry.

"I'm afraid I shall have to go now, Miss Blain. Sue's finished the font and she's waiting for me. Goodbye, and thank you for explaining."

With a parting smile she went swiftly down the church to join Susan.

As soon as they were outside Sue said rather crossly:

"I don't know who your new friend is, Jill, but she's nearly made us late for supper. I'd almost finished the font before you started talking to her. Cook will take a dim view of lateness on Saturday. We'd better run."

Run they did, and just managed to be ready to take their places for the evening meal as the clock started to strike seven. Gillian said nothing to Susan about her talk with Miss Blain, but long after her friend was asleep in the other divan in the Primrose Room she lay wide awake, turning the conversation over in her mind. At last she came to a decision. Slipping quietly out of her divan she knelt beside it and simply asked God to fotgive her sins because the good Shepherd died instead of her, to put His Spirit in her heart, and make her one of the sheep who hears His voice, and loves Him and follows Him.

CHAPTER VIII

THE TALE OF A TOAD

A SQUALL of rain battering against the window of the Primrose Room awoke the two girls. Susan sat up yawning, took one look at the grey skies, and tossing trees, and then promptly snuggled down for another half hour.

"What a beastly day, Jill. It's just as well we shall be in church this morning, anyway."

Gillian got out of bed. She was stricter on discipline than her friend.

"Come on, Susan. There won't be any too much time."

Sue grumbled, but got out of bed fairly promptly.

About two hours later as the girls, clad in macintoshes and carrying umbrellas, walked under the dripping trees down the drive, Gillian started to sing softly, 'The King of Love my Shepherd is, whose goodness faileth never.'

Susan glanced at her curiously and Gillian reddened, but said bravely, "It's true, Sue," and she went on to tell her friend about her talk with Miss Blain, and how she had afterwards given herself to the Good Shepherd, and was going to try to love Him and follow Him always.

Susan listened in uncomfortable silence, and when she spoke at length it was on another subject. She felt vaguely puzzled. It was her prerogative to be the cheerful one, who kept up Gillian's drooping spirits, but this morning, Gillian was the one who was bright and happy.

Once in church, however, Susan began to feel better. The lovely old building, tastefully decorated, and filled with the faint elusive perfume of spring, enfolded her in its security. She enjoyed the service, including the rector's talk on the words, 'The Lord is risen indeed,' and she felt caught up in the glory and triumph of that resurrection morning.

Outside the church she stopped to speak to the school doctor and his wife. Dr. Melsom and Susan had been firm friends ever since she had occupied the sanatorium in solitary state with a bad bout of tonsilitis the previous term.

"I suppose now Miss Francis isn't there to keep an eye on you," he greeted her with a twinkle, "you will be eating all sorts of unsuitable things, and I shall be called in to prescribe some of my special mixture which you enjoyed so much once before."

"Don't tease, Jim," admonished his wife, smiling kindly at Susan. "We were very sorry to hear about Miss Francis's sudden illness, dear. As you and Gillian are on your own, I wondered if you would like to come to tea to-day? I'm afraid we can't offer anything very exciting, but we have some rather good quizzes and Bible games we used to play with the boys."

"Thank you, we would love to come," dimpled Susan who enjoyed games of all kinds, and she hastened to find Gillian and tell her of the invitation.

Gillian had seized the opportunity of Susan's preoccupation with Dr. and Mrs. Melsom, to find Miss Blain and tell her that she was sure now that she was included in the 'My' sheep as well as among the sheep. They were just saying 'Goodbye', having exchanged addresses, and promises to write, when Susan grabbed

Gillian and informed her joyfully that they were going out to tea.

Back at 'Deepdene' cook welcomed the girls with a real 'Sunday dinner', and after they had enjoyed it they settled down to write to their respective parents. They were just about to leave the house for their tea-party when they were startled by the shrill of the telephone bell. Susan and Gillian each raced to answer it, and by means of a little manoeuvring both managed to hear the voice at the other end.

"Miss Pamela speaking. Terrible day, isn't it, but the forecast for to-morrow is good. They promise dry weather and sunshine, and I wondered whether you would like to come for a picnic with Julie, and me, on the moor?"

Susan and Gillian managed to reply in chorus that they would very much like to, thank you.

"We know a lovely sheltered spot below Sadler's Tor," continued Miss Hunter. "Be at Rockleigh by half-past ten, wear warm dresses and blazers, and bring your macs to sit on. We'll come home for tea and afterwards we will go into Swinton and pay a visit to Miss Francis for a few minutes. By the way, I've just been speaking to Mr. and Mrs. Francis, and they tell me that the hospital folk are delighted with their daughter's progress. Goodbye till half-past ten to-morrow, and *don't be late*."

When they had replaced the telephone receiver Susan seized Gillian and whirled her down the hall.

"Tea out to-day, and a picnic on the Moor to-morrow!" she cried gaily. "Even the thought that no brainwave for earning money has visited me fails to depress at this moment."

Mrs. Melsom, mother of four boys, catered largely

for youthful appetites, and the sight of the tea-table at the doctor's house sent Susan's spirits soaring still higher.

There were several kinds of sandwiches, brown, white and currant bread and butter, scones, gingerbread, iced cakes, fruit cake, chocolate biscuits, and fruit salad and cream. As they took their places round the table Susan said with a saucy smile at Dr. Melsom, "Even if I *do* have to take some of your horrible mixture afterwards, I intend to sample something from every plate."

Gillian thought Sue went a little too far sometimes, and she hastened to remark demurely:

"I've always thought a doctor's life must be very interesting. I expect you meet all kinds of odd people, Dr. Melsom?"

"Well," reflected the doctor, "most people are ordinary enough, but one does meet a curious character occasionally."

"The boys used to say their father took notes about them," chimed in Mrs. Melsom, "so that he could write a book, 'Curious characters I have met', when he retires."

"You know I hate writing the shortest letter," protested her husband, "but I do enjoy meeting the 'unusuals', as I call them. I had one in the surgery yesterday morning."

"Tell us," commanded his wife.

"He was an elderly man," began the doctor, "and he'd torn his hand rather badly on a rusty nail. His appearance was spruce and he looked scrupulously clean, so I felt rather surprised when he said he was doing a watchman's job in a lane on the outskirts of Duncombe. I suppose he observed my surprise because he went on to explain that he had worked for the firm in various capacities for years, and when his wife died he took on the job of watchman, being free to go wherever road works were in progress. He says it gives him a chance to see different parts of the country and opportunities for quiet meditation."

"He certainly sounds a most unusual watchman," commented Mrs. Melsom.

"It took some time to fix his hand," continued the doctor, "and he talked away to me. He happened to mention Linfort, my birthplace; said his uncle had a sheep farm on the fells above Linfort, and he often stayed there as a boy."

"That explains how he knows about sheep," put in Gillian, who had not missed a word. "He'd just helped a sheep to get on its feet when I saw him."

She went on to describe her meeting with the old watchman, and to recount his conversation. Susan began to grow bored. She had almost carried out her threat to sample something from every plate, and was eager to start playing games. Sensing her restiveness, Mrs. Melsom suggested an adjournment to the drawing room if everyone had really finished.

"We must allow time to play all the games before the girls have to go," she smiled.

The rules had been explained, and they were just ready to start the first game, when Dr. Melsom was summoned to the telephone.

While waiting for him to return the two girls glanced interestedly round the pleasant drawing-room. Susan's attention was caught and held by a particularly ugly and repulsive china toad seated in solitary state on a corner bracket.

"Hideous, isn't he?" laughed Mrs. Melsom, following the direction of Sue's gaze. "The boys were always saying they couldn't imagine why I kept the thing, but the toad was given to me by my Uncle Stephen, of whom I was very fond. He was a sea captain and, like most sailors, he loved a joke. I remember when he gave me the toad there was a card tied to it with I believe, a quotation from Shakespeare; something about a toad, ugly and venomous having yet a jewel in its head."

Mrs. Mclsom sighed, and looked troubled.

"I'm afraid I let poor Uncle Stephen see I was disappointed, because he usually gave me rather nice birthday presents. I was sorry afterwards. His ship was torpedoed on her next voyage, and I never saw Uncle again."

With her eyes fixed on the toad Mrs. Melsom suddenly stiffened.

"I believe Elsie has chipped it when dusting. She is a good girl, but careless. Please pass it to me, Susan, and I'll see whether it is cracked as well."

With a feeling of revulsion Susan gripped the ugly creature determinedly, the ball of her thumb pressing hard on one of its bulging eyes. To her horror the toad seemed to come alive in her hand. She gave an audible gasp.

"Oh!" she thought wildly, "I've broken the thing."

"It moved," she said tremulously, "the head moved."

"Imagination, dear," laughed Mrs. Melsom. "If the toad had been capable of movement, I'm afraid I should not have kept him so long."

But Susan, calmer now, had discovered the secret. "The head moves when you press hard on his eye. Look!"

Mrs. Melsom looked in amazement as the top of the

toad's head lifted like a lid. The edge of the lid was not smooth and even, and when closed followed the contours and bumps on the toad's skin so perfectly that it was almost impossible to detect the join.

"No wonder I have never noticed it," marvelled Mrs. Melsom, "and I suppose no-one has happened to press that eye so hard. Susan! I believe there is something inside the head."

She inserted two fingers and drew out a tiny packet wrapped in tissue paper. Unfolding it amidst a breathless silence she disclosed a sapphire and diamond pendant.

"Jim!" she called weakly. "Come quickly."

Fortunately Dr. Melsom had finished his telephone call, and could hurry to hear what all the excitement was about.

Susan found herself the heroine of the hour.

When the commotion had subsided somewhat Mrs. Melsom said softly,

"Dear Uncle Stephen. He gave me a lovely birthday present after all. I expect he meant to tell me the toad's secret, if I didn't find it out for myself, but he never came back."

When the two girls had been taken home by Dr. Melsom at the end of the evening, after far too few games for Susan's liking, she remarked to Gillian philosophically,

"Oh well! it doesn't really matter about the games, but it was a nasty moment, Jill, when I thought I'd broken that old toad by grabbing it so hard. It would have been a bit grisly if we'd had to try and replace that as well as Miss Castleton's Dresden Shepherdess."

CHAPTER IX

PICNIC ON THE MOOR

THE girls were thrilled by the prospect of a picnic on the moor, and as soon as they woke next morning rushed to the window to see what weather the day promised. It gave every indication of being fairer even than the forecast, and they dressed in high spirits. Remembering Miss Hunter's injunction they put on warm jersey dresses, Gillian's scarlet, Susan's blue. Gillian pinned on her best brooch. It was a silver and scarlet enamel galleon which had belonged to her mother, and in consequence was a very great treasure.

Wearing blazers and complete with macs Susan and Gillian arrived punctually at Rockleigh Riding School. The picnic basket was just being placed in the back of the car, and in a few minutes they were off.

It was lovely riding through the springtime lanes as they climbed steadily towards the moor. At the top of the last steep hill they paused to give the old car a 'breather' and to survey the panorama spread out before them.

The moor stretched for miles, a study in brown and green and grey; now rising to a hill, now dropping down into a narrow deep valley, or coombe. Rough tracks meandered among the coarse grass and heather, and between whin and bramble bushes. Here and there a patch of vivid green indicated a 'soft spot' or marshy bog. Away to the right Sadler's Tor rose grey and rugged against the skyline.

"We're seeing the moor at its best to-day," sighed Julie Hunter contentedly.

"Yes," agreed her sister, "though it is warm and sunny there is a fresh breeze. In still weather mist comes down very suddenly. I shouldn't like to be caught up here in a mist."

"No," shuddered Gillian. Even in sunshine the moor seemed to her to be a bit forbidding.

As they drove along the wide road across the moor, Susan remarked on the trenches which had been dug at intervals in the stretches of brown ground which they had passed.

"Those are peat bogs," explained Miss Pamela Hunter. "The trenches are where the peat has been cut out and carted away. Some of them are ten and twelve feet deep."

"Nasty places to fall into if you are caught in a mist," supplemented Miss Julie. "It would be almost impossible to climb out again, because the sides would just crumble. You couldn't get foot or hand hold."

Gillian shivered once more and secretly resolved to keep away from the moor unless there was a good stiff breeze blowing which would keep the mist away.

The green saucer-like depression sheltered from the north-east by Sadler's Tor, made an ideal picnic spot. It was carpeted with short sweet turf, which had quickly dried in the sunshine. Macs were spread as precaution against damp, and the picnic basket was brought out from the car.

Hot coffee, sandwiches, sausage rolls, biscuits and fruit tasted delicious in the fresh moorland air. While they were enjoying their repast the two girls told the story of their visit to Mrs. Perry.

"So you are out to earn some money," twinkled Miss

Hunter. "Well, I can give you both a job to-morrow. We have a very full day with pupils, so if you like to come and help groom and clean tack I shall be pleased to pay you suitably."

"Is Brian Timms having a day off, then?" asked Susan.

"Brian Timms is no longer in my employment," said Miss Pamela, with dignity. "I've engaged a girl groom, Linda Lewis, but she can't start until Wednesday."

"I'm glad that boy has gone," rejoiced Susan, little dreaming that he held her responsible for his dismissal. "And we'd like to work at Rockleigh to-morrow, wouldn't we, Jill?"

Gillian agreed emphatically. She loved grooming, and even enjoyed cleaning tack.

After lunch the two Miss Hunters declared their intention of snoozing and sunbathing. This was too slow for energetic Susan, and she persuaded Gillian to go exploring with her.

"We'll look for some new wild flowers and leaves for our Form collection. There are lots of plants up here."

They followed the course of a twisting stream taking care not to stray too far. Gillian was leaning over a rock beside the water to pick a perfect butterfly orchis when she heard a slight tinkle. Intent on securing her prize she took no notice, and a few seconds later added the splendid orchis to her goodly collection of specimens for pressing. When she and Susan returned to the picnic place they found that the sun had sunk behind the tor, and it was quite chilly in the hollow.

Miss Hunter suggested that they should drive home a different way. All was going well until they were about half way to Rockleigh and then something went wrong, and the car slithered to a standstill. It took Julie, with the help of a passing truck driver, almost an hour to get the engine running again, with the result that they had reached Rockleigh with only sufficient time for a 'stand up' tea in hats and coats before rushing off to Swinton to visit Miss Francis.

The schoolmistress was delighted to see each of them and to satisfy herself that Susan and Gillian were safe and well.

By the time the two girls reached the Primrose Room that night they were so tired that they prepared for bed in a kind of daze. Had the moorland air not made them so sleepy Gillian would surely have noticed that her red jersey dress was no longer adorned with her treasured galleon brooch.

CHAPTER X

A BRIEF SEPARATION

DESPITE the fact that the two girls slept heavily because of fatigue, seven o'clock the next morning found them ready for anything. Before they went down to breakfast Susan fished an old purse out of her drawer and suggested that she and Gillian should each put their one pound note in it, towards paying for the Dresden Shepherdess.

"We should be able to manage on our odd money," she suggested. "We haven't had to spend much so far, and we shall only need bus fares to-day."

"That two pounds looks good," gloated Gillian, as she snapped the purse shut. "When we come home to-night we shall be able to add whatever Miss Hunter decides we have been worth to-day. I wonder how much it will be. Anyhow, it's lovely to think we shall be enjoying ourselves, and earning money at the same time."

At the end of a busy, happy day at Rockleigh Miss Hunter declared that the girls had earned ten shillings each.

"You've been a splendid help," she told them. "No," as they protested modestly at her generosity, "it isn't a bit too much. You've thoroughly earned every penny of it. Now, how would you like to earn some more money to-morrow? Not here, of course, because Linda Lewis is coming, but somewhere else?"

"Just give us the chance," dimpled Susan, "and we shall be right on the job."

"You may not like it," warned Miss Pamela with a

twinkle, "because it's tedious work, and your fingers will get badly stained, but I can give you permission to do it. Mr. Cunliffe, our friend who owns Rockleigh Nurseries, is needing help with picking the side shoots off his tomato plants. He pays two shillings and ninepence an hour and thinks he could legitimately employ you for a few hours. If you would like to try the job I will 'phone him now, and tell him to expect you in the morning."

The lure of two and ninepence an hour was not to be resisted, and both girls agreed eagerly to place their services at Mr. Cunliffe's disposal.

They returned joyfully to Deepdene with another pound note to add to the two already in the old purse, and the prospect of earning more money the next day.

Cook readily agreed to give them breakfast in time to allow them to reach Rockleigh by half-past eight. She was secretly relieved that they were going to spend another whole day there, as the responsibility for the two girls in Miss Francis's absence weighed heavily on herself and Lucy.

"I wonder whether we ought to tell Cook what we intend doing?" ventured Gillian uneasily, while they were preparing for bed in the Primrose Room.

"Not necessary," declared Susan stoutly, "seeing that Miss Hunter has given us permission. Anyway, we shall be having our riding lesson after lunch, so at least we'll be doing what cook thinks we are for part of the day."

At five and twenty minutes past eight Susan and Gillian presented themselves, rather timidly at the gate of Rockleigh Nurseries. Mr. Cunliffe greeted them kindly and took them himself to one of the big greenhouses.

"I thought you might like to be here together," he said. "One of you can work down the right hand side and one down the left, and then you won't get in each other's way. Now this is what I want you to do."

Carefully he showed the girls which side shoots to take from the plants, and after watching them for a few minutes to make sure they understood, he hurried off to attend to other work.

It was warm and steamy in the greenhouse and the job was certainly tedious. Before long the girls' fingers were badly stained, but they worked steadily on, and were more than half way along the rows of plants when a welcome diversion occurred. The door was pushed open, and a jolly-looking land girl carrying a tray stepped inside.

"We have a quarter of an hour break about eleven," she smiled, "so I thought you might like a cup of tea and a cheese roll. You can rinse your hands under the tap outside, and sit on the step in the sunshine while you eat."

Gratefully Susan and Gillian accepted the tray, and adopted both suggestions.

"Help!" exclaimed Gillian as she sank down on the step, "I hadn't realised how my feet ached, but I'm liking it, aren't you, Sue?"

Susan grimaced eloquently. "I wouldn't go as far as to say that, but the thought of that two and nine-pence an hour keeps me going." Hungrily she took a large bite out of her cheese roll.

By twenty minutes to one every plant had received attention, and the two girls were surveying their work with conscious pride when Mr. Cunliffe arrived to pass judgment.

"You've done well," he approved, "and I should

like to have you again to-morrow. Are you free to come?"

Both girls nodded briefly, so he continued: "Now shall I pay you for this morning, or would you like two day's wages to-morrow?"

"We'd like to have it all together, please," agreed the girls as they said 'Goodbye'.

They hurried along to the riding school, because Miss Pamela had invited them to one o'clock lunch in the bungalow, to meet the new girl groom.

Both Susan and Gillian liked Linda Lewis on sight. She was plump, pleasant and placid, and looked the embodiment of easy good-nature, but that did not prevent her from being an accomplished horsewoman. After Susan had watched her at the jumps she gazed at her with increased respect.

"I think Miss Lewis is a great improvement on Brian Timms," Susan confided to Miss Pamela as they rode out of the stable yard a little later.

Miss Hunter was pleased that they liked Linda.

"She is certainly much better suited to riding school work, though Brian Timms had a wonderful way with unbroken horses. I believe he is working temporarily at a farm on the Minchington road but his idea is to get a job at that stud on the moor where they break in ponies. I'd give him a reference for that work if he asked me. Now," turning to the other three riding behind, "I think we'll take the bridle paths as far as the lane beside Clows Farm, and come back by the river."

When Susan and Gillian reached Deepdene that evening they found a hot supper awaiting them both, and something else waiting for Gillian.

"A letter from Dad," she cried joyfully, pouncing

on it and ripping open the envelope. While she read the short note a variety of expressions chased one another across her face.

"It's perfectly lovely of Dad to think of it," she murmured, "but oh! dear it will mean letting you down, Sue. Here, read it."

She thrust the sheet of paper into Susan's hands.

"Dear Gillian," read Susan obediently. "My business journeying will bring me into your neighbourhood to-morrow, and give me the opportunity of spending a couple of days with you. I propose to call for you at ten o'clock in the morning and take you with me to Minchington, where I have reserved rooms at Mounts Hotel. My business in Minchington will not take long, so we can go around a bit, and then I can drop you at school again, in three days time. I'm afraid it is a case of 'short and sweet', but may make up a little for our cancelled holiday. Be sure to be ready at ten, dear, as I have an appointment in Minchington.

Love, from

Your own Daddy."

"Of course it will be lovely to see Daddy," Gillian looked troubled as her friend handed back the letter, "but I shall hate leaving you alone, Sue. If I'd known in time I might have asked Dad to include you."

"He doesn't want me," said Susan, trying her best to sound cheerful. "Go and enjoy yourself, Jill, and don't worry about me."

But Gillian looked even more worried. "Oh!" she cried, remembering, "the tomato plants!"

"What about the tomato plants?" retorted Susan calmly. "If I'm to be on my own I shall be at a loose end, and I intend to ask Mr. Cunliffe to let me work all day."

Gillian was not consoled.

"But it seems terrible to let you earn my share of the money, Sue, though I can't very well disappoint Dad."

Susan playfully tweaked Gillian's short brown hair.

"I said, don't worry. You needn't flatter yourself I shall miss you," she dimpled. "I'm going to be far too busy."

Satisfied that Susan really didn't mind her going, Gillian packed a small case in a whirl of excitement, and gave herself up to the joys of anticipation.

When prayers had been said in the Primrose Room that night, and the occupants of the twin divans were having their usual goodnight talk, Susan made a proposal.

"If Mr. Cunliffe agrees to let me work all day to-morrow," she began, "we should have enough money to buy the Shepherdess. Would you mind very much, Jill, if I go to Rocombe on Thursday morning and get her from Mrs. Perry? It will be something else for me to do while you're away."

"Of course, you must go and buy the Shepherdess," cried Gillian eagerly. "If you've done most of the hard work it's only fair you should have the fun of receiving the prize. That at least, will be easy."

"You've said it," grinned Susan. "Just a question of 'bringing home the bacon'."

Though in actual fact it was to prove not so easy, after all,

CHAPTER XI

THE SHEPHERDESS SECURED

NEXT morning Gillian walked with Susan down the drive to, as she put it, set the worker on her way. Fortunately, cook had insisted on providing Susan with a picnic lunch.

"We mustn't let Miss Hunter supply all your meals," she said a trifle severely. "Miss Francis would not approve of that, I'm sure."

When the moment of parting came, Gillian waved until Susan disappeared round the bend of the road, then went back to await with what patience she could muster, the arrival of her father. Her patience was not tried too hard, for he arrived early, and father and daughter were soon off on their brief holiday.

They sped along in the car talking busily until they reached the main Minchington road when Gillian thought she had better be quiet and not distract her father from his driving. Just ahead of them the Minchington bus was travelling towards a 'request' stop some yards distant. Glancing idly out of the car window Gillian caught sight of a would-be passenger trying desperately to catch up with the bus. This old gentleman carried a small case in a bandaged hand, and with a start Gillian realised that it was her friend, the watchman. There happened to be nobody waiting at the stop and the bus went serenely on its way.

"Dad!" said Gillian, "could you please stop a minute? The watchman has missed the bus."

Mr. Dacre raised a surprised eyebrow, but good-naturedly steered the car into a convenient lay-by and stopped.

"What's all this about a watchman?" he asked.

Gillian gave a brief account of her meeting with the watchman and his visit to Dr. Melsom's surgery, ending with the words, "He is *very* respectable, really Dad. Dr. Melsom liked him."

"In that case," said her father gravely, though his eyes smiled, "we can hardly leave him stranded. Fortunately we have a few minutes in hand. You'd better run back, dear, and offer your friend a lift."

As Gillian piloted him, after a little persuasion, back to the car she murmured shyly, "I remember what you said about the sheep, and I thought you'd like to know I can say now the Lord is my shepherd."

The old watchman beamed and he nodded well-pleased, but, as they had reached the waiting vehicle, he addressed himself to Mr. Dacre.

"Thank you, kindly, sir. I'm meeting my nephew in Minchington, and we're catching a train at junction for a few days' fishing together. Job in Duncombe is finished, and new one is in the next county."

On they went again, Gillian feeling glad she had seen the watchman as he was going away, and that it was a good start to a holiday to give a fellow traveller a lift.

Meanwhile, Susan was working her way slowly down one side of a greenhouse at Rockleigh Nursery. Mr. Cunliffe, after a good deal of persuasion had agreed to employ her for the whole day. She was to work from nine until one, and from half-past two till half-past five.

At one o'clock Susan seized her picnic lunch and hurried along to Rockleigh Riding School. For conscience sake she must spend a little time there.

Miss Pamela greeted her with a teasing smile.

"Come and give an account of yourself," she invited. "It's a blessing Mr. Cunliffe collected his small daughter after her riding lesson, so that I knew you were working there again, otherwise I might have made a bad blunder. I was on the point of telephoning 'Deepdene' to ask whether you would like to come to the gymkhana at Swinton to-morrow afternoon."

"Oh!" exclaimed Susan, "I should have had to confess *then* to cook what we've been up to, but I'd love to come to the gymkhana."

"What about Gillian? Where is she, by the way?"

Susan explained that Gillian had gone with her father for a few days' holiday, but would be back again on Friday.

"You must have some coffee with us," said Miss Pamela kindly, as Susan unwrapped her packet of sandwiches.

While they all sat enjoying their coffee they discussed the forthcoming gymkhana.

"I'm going to Rocombe in the morning to buy the Shepherdess," Sue told Miss Hunter, "but that won't take very long."

"My! You've soon scraped five pounds together," laughed Miss Julie.

"Well, we shan't actually have it until I finish work to-day, and that reminds me I ought to be getting back." Susan rose with the words.

"We shall be leaving here at half-past two to-morrow," Miss Pamela reminded her, "and please don't be late. I particularly want to see the first event."

"I'll be here by half-past two," promised Sue as she ran off.

She worked doggedly through the afternoon in the warm damp atmosphere of the greenhouse, standing first on one tired foot and then on the other. Her fingers were becoming expert now and by five and twenty minutes past five she had completed her task. She was checking to make sure she had not missed a plant when Mr. Cunliffe looked in.

"You've stuck it well, and done a fine job," he complimented her. "Now comes the best part, your wages. I owe twenty-two shillings for the work you and your friend did yesterday, and you must have a pound for to-day. So that's two guineas, and I'm much obliged for your help."

Susan joyfully tucked the two pound notes and two shilling piece into the middle division of her purse, and washed the worst of the stains from her fingers.

"I don't mind if I never see another tomato plant," she thought wearily, as she trudged to the bus stop. "But it's been worth it, to get the five pounds made up."

The consciousness of the money in her purse gave her an excited feeling. To-morrow she could actually go to Rocombe and buy the Dresden Shepherdess.

She enjoyed her hot supper at seven o'clock, but decided to go to bed directly afterwards, and read her new book for an hour.

It seemed strange in the Primrose Room without Gillian, but she was almost too tired to mind. Before she had been in bed ten minutes the book slid from her fingers and she was fast asleep.

A shaft of strong sunlight falling across her face awakened her next morning, but while she was eating her breakfast it began to rain.

Lucy came in with a packet of sandwiches, and a decidedly disapproving expression.

"Cook has made you a picnic lunch as you said Miss Hunter had given you permission to go to Rocombe, but if I may say so, Miss, it isn't picnic weather. The forecast said heavy showers this morning, though brightening later, and probably a fine afternoon. You'll do yourself no end of harm sitting on damp grass."

"Oh! I'm not going to do that," Susan promptly assured her. "I'm really going to visit a friend of Miss Hunter's, and I shall have my lunch with her. Then I shall go on to the gymkhana."

By half-past eleven Susan was walking down the lane to 'Twin Gables', the purse containing the precious five pounds clasped tightly in her hand. There had been two or three heavy showers while she was in the bus and another overtook her just as she reached the gate of Mrs. Perry's cottage.

"Come in," beamed its owner, hospitably, as she answered Susan's ring, "you are just in time. Hang your mac here in the entry, dear. Rufus will be just as pleased as I am to see you."

"I'm afraid I haven't come to stay long," apologised Susan, "but I thought perhaps you would let me eat my lunch here."

She pulled the packet of sandwiches out of her macintosh pocket. "By the way, I've brought the money for the Dresden Shepherdess."

"My! you've soon managed to get it together. Eat your lunch here and welcome, and I'll make you a nice cup of hot chocolate." Mrs. Perry chuckled. "I've a weakness for hot chocolate myself, though I expect plump folk like me ought not to drink it."

They were soon sitting over a cosy meal in the kitchen and while they enjoyed it Susan told Mrs.

Perry about the gymkhana she was hoping to attend that afternoon.

"If you have to be at Rockleigh by half-past two I mustn't keep you," said Mrs. Perry rising as soon as the meal ended, and fetching the Dresden Shepherdess. She rolled the little figure carefully in white tissue and brown paper, and handed her to Susan in exchange for the five pounds.

"I shall miss my Shepherdess, of course," smiled Mrs. Perry sadly, "but five pounds is worth much more to me at the moment. Now don't stop coming to see me because you have got what you wanted. Come again soon, and bring Gillian with you next time."

Mrs. Perry and Rufus stood at the gate, and watched Susan run along the lane.

CHAPTER XII

A SHOCK FOR SUSAN

THERE was no direct bus service between Rocombe and Rockleigh so Susan decided to take the Duncombe bus to Thatchford Corner, and walk across two fields to the Minchington road. More than one bus route from Minchington ran through Rockleigh, and she thought if she walked along the main road a bus would be bound to overtake her fairly soon.

She reached the Minchington road without delay and had walked a short distance when she came to a farm separated from the busy road by the space of a small field. A cart track led from an open gateway to the farm entrance on the far side of the field, and on a board nailed to a post, 'Southernwood Farm' was painted in white letters.

"I like that name," thought Susan, glancing again at the pretty building with thatched roof and deep-set windows. Then she saw that a toddler was running along the cart track, unsteadily but purposefully, evidently bent on getting out into the road. There appeared to be nobody else about, so if the child was to be stopped it seemed to be up to Susan. Realising she would probably need two hands for the job she looked round for a safe place in which to dump the Shepherdess. To one side of the open gateway stood a Dutch barn half filled with trusses of hay. Susan laid her precious burden on the hay, and swooped to the attack. The toddler was only a few yards from the gateway when she grabbed him and barred his further progress. He set up a tornado of shrieks as she picked him up, and carried him, kicking and struggling towards the farm.

Half-way along the track she was met by a pale distraught young woman, gasping as she ran. She snatched the small boy from Susan and hugged him tightly.

"Oh, Robin!" she said brokenly, "who could have left the garden gate open? Robin, it was naughty of you to run away."

She turned to Robin's rescuer with a wavering but very warm smile.

"I don't know how to thank you, dear," she said gratefully, "I thought Robin was with his Daddy, and than I saw him from an upstairs window running along the track. I raced down, but I could never have reached him in time, and," she shuddered, "the traffic on that road never ceases."

Hot with embarrassment Susan cut short her repeated thanks, and refused offers of refreshment in the farmhouse. She said a firm goodbye and hurried towards the gateway, but before she could reach it a lorry turned in, and she saw that the driver was Brian Timms. He stopped the lorry, called to her, and made as though to jump out.

To Susan there seemed something menacing in his attitude, and in blind panic she fled across the field, climbed the fence, and ran along the road. She heard a bus coming, and turning, signalled frantically. The bus stop was still some yards ahead, but the driver good-naturedly pulled up, and Susan scrambled aboard. Fortunately it happened to be the right bus, and when Susan had paid her fare she smoothed her untidy hair. There was room for only one thought in her mind. She had successfully dodged Timms, but in spite of her promise she was going to be frightfully late at Rockleigh, and Miss Pamela would be exceedingly angry with her.

Indeed, Miss Hunter was angry. In curt tones she bade Susan get into the waiting car, adding icily, "After promising to be here in time, you might have made an effort, Susan. I've been waiting here nearly an hour."

Already considerably shaken, Susan now felt completely crushed. She sat silent, weighed down by the thought that her conduct must appear unappreciative of Miss Hunter's kindness in taking her to Swinton.

On arrival at the gymkhana ground, however, things took a turn for the better. It had been found necessary to alter the programme slightly, and the event Miss Hunter particularly wished to see had not yet taken place. This news banished the last traces of her annoyance, which had been gradually diminishing during the journey from Rockleigh. She told Susan she could consider herself forgiven and she must cheer up and enjoy the show.

Susan's drooping spirits promptly revived, and she became completely absorbed as one thrilling event succeeded another. The standard of riding was high, and the jumping particularly good.

A girl of about Susan's own age won the cup, completing the round of the course without a single fault.

"I shan't think I can jump, after that," thought Susan ruefully.

Miss Hunter insisted that they have the best tea the refreshment marquee could provide, and she brought

Susan a mammoth ice afterwards. This finally convinced Sue that all was now well between them.

They stayed until the end of the gymkhana, and then Miss Hunter suggested that they should pay a flying visit to Miss Francis, as they were in Swinton, and it was the evening visiting hour.

The invalid was delighted to see them. Her progress had been maintained, and she was beginning to talk of leaving hospital.

Miss Hunter told her about the gymkhana in such spirited and interesting fashion, that Miss Francis declared she had enjoyed it almost as much as though she, herself, had been a spectator. Susan lost her awe of the sixth-form mistress sufficiently to give a dramatic account of the discovery of the lovely pendant in Mrs. Melsom's ugly china toad. Miss Francis listened attentively, and greeted the climax with gratifying astonishment.

"I'm very glad," she smiled. "Mrs. Melsom is so kind and nice, and with four sons to educate I don't suppose she has been able to have many trinkets. It will give her pleasure to remember that she treasured the toad because it was given to her by her Uncle Stephen even though she had no idea it was more than a rather ugly piece of china."

When Miss Hunter and Susan rose to leave, the invalid said surprisingly, with a mischievous twinkle,

"You seem to be passing your time quite pleasantly, Susan. Don't have all the adventures before I am there to enjoy some with you."

At length Miss Hunter deposited a tired but happy Susan at her own front door, and left with fervent expressions of gratitude ringing in her ears.

It was not until Susan was preparing for bed alone

in the Primrose Room that she realised with numbing shock that, in her anxiety to escape from Brian Timms, she had forgotten all about her parcel. The Dresden Shepherdess, for which she and Gillian had worked so hard, lay abandoned in a Dutch barn at Southernwood Farm on the Minchington road.

CHAPTER XIII

MISSING

FOR a paralysing moment Susan stood, hairbrush in hand, transfixed by this awful truth. Then common sense came to her aid. After all, nobody but herself knew that the little parcel was lying on the hay. She had only to walk the three miles to Southernwood Farm and collect it, then all would be well.

Wide awake now, and desperately anxious to retrieve the Dresden Shepherdess, she wondered whether she dare go to-night. The longer she waited, the less chance of the parcel being recovered.

Softly she drew back the bolts of the fire escape door and stepped out on to the iron platform. There was no moon; everything was dark and absolutely still. Not a rustle or whisper broke the eerie silence.

As her eyes grew accustomed to the dimness she realized that a mist was creeping up to her, and looking down she saw it eddying thinly in the void below. For a time she stood in the silence and darkness trying to summon courage to face the three mile walk alone.

While Susan hesitated on the fire escape platform, the mist grew thicker and thicker until she realised the folly of turning out in its clammy embrace. She closed and bolted the fire escape door and began to prepare for bed.

"I'll go as soon as it's light," she told herself. "The mist should have gone by then. If I bump my head five times on the pillow I ought to wake up at five o'clock.

That will give me plenty of time to get to Southernwood Farm and back before breakfast."

The pillow-bumping proved effective, for by a quarter to five Susan was fully awake. As soon as the window began to grow really light she quickly and quietly washed and dressed. Very gently she drew back the bolts of the fire escape door, closed it softly behind her, and tiptoed down the iron stairs. The mist had almost vanished.

She ran down the drive and out into the road empty and silent at this hour. A breeze was stirring now, and as it strengthened it dispersed the remnants of mist still lingering in the hollows, and above the fields beside the river. Her footsteps echoed loudly as she hurried along past sleeping houses, and soon she had left the town behind.

There were few cars as yet on the busy Minchington road, but several lorries passed Susan and their drivers looked curiously at the solitary pedestrian. As the time passed she met farm-workers cycling or walking to work, and once she had to wait beside a farm entrance while a herd of cows were driven in for milking. By the time she reached the Dutch barn which was her goal the countryside had fully wakened to life.

Susan remembered quite clearly where she had put the Shepherdess and she went confidently forward to pick up the parcel. But to her dismay, there was no parcel there. Could she have been mistaken about the exact spot? She looked on all the surrounding trusses and now thoroughly alarmed dug down between them, probing in to the hay with frantic fingers. At last she was forced to realise that the parcel was not in the Dutch barn at all. The Shepherdess, which represented not only her work and money but Gillian's also, had completely vanished.

For a few moments Susan stood, overcome by the calamity, wondering what further steps to take. She felt certain that she had covered every possible spot where she could have placed the Shepherdess.

"I'll go and see whether it could have been seen from the road," she murmured.

Satisfied that the parcel could not have been spotted by anyone passing along the road, but would have been plainly visible to a passer-by on the track to the farm, her brow cleared.

"That's the explanation," she decided with relief, "the parcel was evidently picked up by one of the farm people. When I explain that it belongs to me I'm sure they will return it."

Buoyed up by this hopeful thought, Susan went cheerfully up the cart track to the farm.

The farmer's wife, Robin's mother, was just coming out of the dairy, and she greeted Susan with a smile of delighted recognition.

"Good morning, dear. You're an early visitor. What can I do for you?"

Susan explained about the parcel she had left in the Dutch barn, and asked eagerly whether it had been picked up and taken to the farm.

"I haven't heard of anyone finding a parcel in the Dutch barn," the farmer's wife said thoughtfully, "it certainly wasn't found by myself or my husband. But come and sit down in the kitchen, dear, and I'll get my husband to question all the workers."

As she led Susan into the kitchen she asked if she might know what to call her, and added that her own name was Mrs. Newton. Having established her young visitor in a comfortable chair and insisted on her drinking a glass of milk and eating a slice of bread spread with farm butter and honey, she went off to see her husband who would question his 'hands'. Presently, Farmer Newton returned himself and said that nobody had seen the parcel.

"I've asked everybody except Brian Timms, and he isn't here to ask." Farmer Newton's brow darkened. "That youth has let me down properly. Said he'd be here early, because I gave him yesterday evening off to go over the moor to that stud to see about a job there. For my pains he hasn't turned up this morning. I've no time for people who leave one in the lurch."

Full of his own grievance the farmer scarcely noticed Susan's stricken expression.

"Thank you for asking about my parcel," she managed to say, "and thank you for the milk, but I must go now or I'll be late back."

With a heavy heart Sue trudged back to the road. What would Gillian think of her carelessness?

Alternately walking and running, she made the return journey to 'Deepdene' in record time. Lucy met her at the front door. Assuming that Susan was in the garden, she was just coming out to tell her that breakfast was waiting.

CHAPTER XIV

A TIMELY RESCUE

AS the clock struck ten, the sound of a car stopping outside the front door brought Susan into the hall. Gillian came flying up the steps calling urgently:

"Sue! Sue! come and speak to Dad. He can only stay a few minutes."

Susan rushed out with her friend to the car to be proudly introduced to the tall dark man with a charming smile, who was Gillian's father.

Mr. Dacre talked pleasantly to the two girls for ten minutes, presented each with a box of chocolates, and then said he must really be on his way once more.

Susan and Gillian stood waving until the car rounded the bend in the drive, and as they turned to go back into the house Susan took a deep breath thinking, "*Now* I must tell Jill."

Before she could speak, however, Gillian said soberly, though with no trace of her old 'tragedy queen' air,

"Sue, something awful has happened."

Susan gasped. It seemed like telepathy or second sight. *She* should have been saying that, not Gillian.

"You remember when we went for that picnic on the moor," continued Gillian, not noticing Susan's peculiar expression, "and I wore my galleon brooch? Well, I think I must have lost it while we were looking for wild flowers. I know it was still on my dress at lunch time, because Miss Julie made some remark about it. We were so tired when we went to bed that night that I didn't miss my brooch, but it couldn't have been on the dress then because it wasn't there when I unpacked at the hotel. Subconsciously I realised I hadn't seen it when I put the dress in the case."

Gillian looked so upset that Susan felt it was not the moment to mention the loss of the Dresden Shepherdess. Relieved that she could put off the moment of confession she said sympathetically, "Don't worry, Jill. We'll ask cook to pack us a picnic lunch, and get Miss Hunter's permission to go on the Moor. If we search all the ground we covered looking for wild flowers we shall be bound to find your brooch. It's too early in the year for many visitors to be wandering over the moor, so it's unlikely that anyone will have found it in the meantime."

Miss Hunter, however, was at first unwilling to give permission for the expedition.

"The people at the stud 'phoned me last night on business," she said, "and they told me it was very misty then, I can't allow you on the moor if there is mist about. However, hold the line here, and I'll go into the office to 'phone, and ask them what weather conditions are like now."

Susan and Gillian took it in turns to hold the telephone receiver, and after what seemed an age Miss Hunter returned to say,

"It's all right, you can go. The stud folk assure me there is no mist at the moment, and a wind is blowing which will keep it away for to-day, at any rate. I hope you find the brooch. 'Phone when you get safely back, and we'll arrange about picking you up this evening to visit Miss Francis. Bye-bye for now."

Susan consulted her bus timetable and found they

could just catch a bus to Moorend, a village almost on the moor. Three-quarters of an hour later they alighted from the bus in Moorend and turned up the short steep lane which led on to the moor.

Half-way along this lane two cottages stood side by side. They were picturesque dwellings with thatched roofs, and on a ladder set against one of them a thatcher was busy. Gillian and Susan stood watching his patient skilful weaving until Gillian, anxious to start looking for her brooch, dragged her friend away.

On the edge of the moor they took a survey.

"I can see the peat bog over there," Gillian said. "We have to go along beside it to get to Sadler's Tor."

"Let's find your brooch first," Susan advised, "and then have lunch in the hollow below the Tor."

They stepped out briskly and had almost reached the peat bog when Susan clutched Gillian's arm.

"Listen!" she commanded. "I heard something."

They stood still, listening, and as they waited the sound came again, a faint cry of, "Help!"

"It seemed to come out of the ground," said Gillian, puzzled.

Susan darted forward along the track, then swerved to the left where one of the trenches had been cut in the peat bog. Standing at a safe distance from the edge she peered over and looked down into the white strained face of Brian Timms. He stared back as though scarcely able to believe she was real.

"I thought nobody would ever come," he croaked. "I've called till I'm hoarse. I walked into this in the mist last night, and I can't get out."

"Are you hurt?" asked Susan anxiously. The trench was about twelve feet deep.

"No, the ground is soft and sort of spongy. That's

partly why I haven't been able to climb out. I can't get any grip with my feet, and the sides don't give a hand-hold either. They just break away. I've been trying for hours, and I'm all in."

Gillian, who had joined Susan on the brink of the trench, was afraid he was going to faint.

This was a very different Brian from the bold, bumptious, insolent youth they knew.

"He must be starving," she said, pityingly. "Give him some of our lunch, Sue. I'm going to run back and ask the thatcher to bring his ladder. That's what we need, a ladder."

"Yes, go and ask him," approved Susan. "You can run faster than I can. But before you go, give me your belt to join to mine so that I can lower some food and coffee to Brian."

Gillian sped off to enlist the aid of the thatcher and his ladder while Susan lowered first the small flask of coffee, and then a packet of sandwiches, to the prisoner in the trench. He ate and drank eagerly, and when he had finished looked up with a smile that was neither mocking nor familiar, but grateful and friendly.

"You've just about saved my life," he said simply. "I'd had nothing since dinner yesterday. I wouldn't wait for tea because I wanted to get across to the stud after a job. I've got it too, if Miss Hunter will give me a reference. D'you think she will?" he asked almost humbly.

"I'm sure she will," Susan assured him, remembering what Miss Hunter had said about his suitability for the work of schooling ponies.

"She's a good sort, and so are you," said Brian Timms fervently and unexpectedly. Then he added with a sheepish grin, "I've got something which I think belongs to you, and the first thing I do when I get out of here is to bring it back to you."

"Oh!" cried Susan quickly. "You mean the parcel I left in the Dutch barn? You found it?"

Brian nodded and started to speak but Susan interrupted to ask in tones of anguish, "Did you realise it was fragile?"

"Naturally I looked at what I'd found." There was just a hint of the old swagger in his tone. "It's in a safe place, so don't worry. You've got something worth having there, I can tell you."

Before another word could be spoken the sound of heavy footsteps broke the silence. Susan saw two men approaching across the moor, carrying a ladder, Gillian hurrying along beside them. In a few minutes the thatcher and his friend were looking down at Brian Timms.

"You're in a bit of a fix seemingly," the thatcher's small blue eyes twinkled, "but we'll soon 'ave 'ee out of it. 'Tis lucky for you this little maid remembered I was working close handy with a ladder."

Assisted by his friend he lowered the ladder into the trench, and the two men held it steady while Brian climbed out.

"'Tis just as well you're nimble, lad," said the thatcher's friend, as the ladder was hauled up again. "Ladder would soon 'ave sunk in that soft ground."

Brian Timms looked round at the little group and said gratefully, "I don't know how to thank you all. Here wait, I'll help carry that ladder."

He turned to Susan as the three moved off carrying the ladder between them.

"I shall be up at 'Deepdene' later with that parcel," he promised.

CHAPTER XV

SUSAN MAKES A RESOLUTION

"WHAT did he mean, Sue, about bringing a parcel?" asked Gillian curiously, as the two girls crossed the moor.

"I'll tell you while we are walking the rest of the way to the Tor," Susan promised.

Now that the Dresden Shepherdess was to be restored to them, Susan was nothing loth to tell how nearly they had lost her, and she plunged into a dramatic account of the happenings of the past two days.

"I'm glad you stopped young Robin from rushing out into the road, anyway," said Gillian, when the tale ended. "It would have been awful if he'd run under a lorry, or something. Well, here we are at our picnic spot. I expect you'd like to have lunch before we start looking for my brooch," she suggested unselfishly.

"You mean what's *left* of the lunch," laughed Susan. "We shall have to tighten our belts before we start."

"We'll pretend we're slimming," cried Gillian gaily, "and I believe I've read somewhere that fresh air is filling."

Susan glanced sideways at her friend. Jill had certainly changed. The old Gillian would have been lamenting that fresh air made one ravenous, and there was hardly anything to eat. Her moods and fits of depression were things of the past, and she had quite lost what Susan used to describe as her 'tragedy queen' airs. Now, as she set out the meagre repast, Gillian was singing softly, 'I've found a friend, oh such a friend. He loved me ere I knew Him.' She indicated the lunch with a flourish. "There it is, Sue. We'll eat it slowly to make it last."

Susan looked thoughtful and troubled as she bit into a sandwich. She wished she knew the Friend that Gillian seemed so happy to have found.

"I'm sure Jill changed after that talk she had with Miss Blain while we were decorating the church," she mused. "It's all tied up with the verses Miss Francis read about the Good Shepherd, on the first night of the hols. Jill's tried to talk of it more than once, but I've always changed the subject. To-night when we go to bed I'll steer the conversation round to Miss Blain, and get Jill to tell me just what happened."

"Sue, you're forgetting to eat," Gillian rallied her. "If you don't watch out I shall take more than my share."

"I'll see you don't," Susan realised suddenly that she was hungry and fell to with zest.

"While we've been eating," said Gillian a few minutes later, "I've been thinking back to when we were here before, and I've remembered something. When I leaned over to pick that butterfly orchis I heard a metallic little clink. I took no notice then, but now I'm wondering whether it could have been my brooch falling against a stone."

"Quite possible," opined Sue, alert and interested in a minute. "The butterfly orchis was growing on one of the banks of that little stream. As soon as we've finished we will make our way there. You go up-stream and I'll go down, and we'll look under every blade of grass, so to speak."

A short time later they separated on the bank of the stream to walk their different ways. Slowly, Gillian worked her way up-stream while Susan worked down, and soon they were some distance apart. Suddenly a joyful shout rent the air and Susan turned to see her friend waving something that gleamed in the sunlight.

"Good! Jill's found it," she exclaimed, rushing to congratulate her.

"I feel like the woman with the ten pieces of silver when she found her piece that was lost," exulted Gillian, as she pinned the galleon brooch securely on her dress, and fastened the safety catch.

"I'll play the part of the neighbours and rejoice with you," dimpled Susan, "but just at the moment we had better concentrate on hurrying. If we don't wish to arrive in Moorend in time to miss a bus, and wait two hours for the next, we shall have to run most of the way back."

They caught the bus with only a few minutes to spare and immediately on arrival back at 'Deepdene' telephoned Miss Hunter to advise her of their safe return.

"I'm delighted you found the brooch," she said as soon as she heard the news. "I don't mind telling you now that I thought you had embarked on a wild goose chase. Julie and I will call for you both at half-past six and take you with us to see Miss Francis."

Lucy told the girls that as they would be going into Swinton cook would give them high tea at five o'clock instead of supper at seven. Then they could have light supper last thing.

"Help!" exclaimed Susan hungrily, "a whole hour to wait. Bless your father, Jill, for giving us these boxes of chocolates. Without a few chocs to fortify us we should be fainting by the wayside before five o'clock."

The two strolled out on to the terrace and sat down in the sunshine their precious boxes of chocolates beside them. For a short time they munched in companionable silence then Susan said diffidently:

"Jill, I hope you won't mind if I ask you something? I was going to save it for our 'Goodnight' talk, but after visiting Miss Francis and a late supper, we may be too sleepy."

"Ask me anything you like, Sue." Gillian bit into a hard chocolate, and smiled lazily at her friend.

"Well, this is going to sound a bit rude, but it's true. I took a dim view of spending the holidays at school with you. I'd always thought you were moody, and a bit of a tragedy queen, and I felt it would be tough being cheerful for two, but you've changed, Jill. You're quite different, and it seems to me it's since you had that talk with Miss Blain when we were doing the flowers. I wondered if you would tell me what happened."

In her own words Gillian gave the substance of her conversation with the rector's sister, and added, a dreamy expression in her dark eyes,

"I think I'd always believed in a vague sort of way that the Lord Jesus Christ died for the sin of the world. I didn't believe until then that He died because of my sin; instead of me. I couldn't rest till I had asked God to forgive me for His sake, and help me to love Him and follow Him always. I've felt so safe and happy since."

"Thank you for telling me," said Susan, after a brief pause. Then she went on to talk of what they would do during the rest of the holidays. Sue didn't find it easy to speak about the deeper things of life, but Gillian felt it would not be long before Sue, too, became one of the sheep who know the Shepherd's voice, and love Him and follow Him.

Just before the two girls sat down to their long-awaited high tea Brian Timms arrived with the parcel containing the Dresden Shepherdess.

"It's a nice piece," he said as he handed the package to Susan. "My uncle keeps one of the antique shops in Duncombe, and he's interested in Dresden china."

"Is he, indeed?" muttered Sue as Brian retreated down the drive. "It looks as though he could have disposed of his booty all right. I don't know what you think, Jill, but I should say it's a mercy Brian Timms took a toss into that peat bog. Otherwise we might have lost our Shepherdess for ever."

CHAPTER XVI

RED LETTER DAYS

MISS FRANCIS greeted her visitors in great excitement when they walked into the ward that evening. The nurse in charge kindly allowed all four to go in together for a few minutes so that the patient could tell them her good news.

"Doctor said this morning I can go home to-morrow," she informed them joyfully.

"Does home mean 'Deepdene' or your own home?" enquired Miss Hunter.

"'Deepdene', of course. Mother has been pressing me to go home for a week, but I undertook to stay at school, and I should feel I'd failed badly if I deserted my post. I want to be at 'Deepdene' for a little while before Miss Castleton returns."

"You haven't failed," smiled Miss Julie. "You could hardly help being taken ill. Now would you like me to bring the car and collect you in the morning? I can get your suitcase of clothes from 'Deepdene' when we run the girls home to-night."

Arrangements had just been made for them to be at the hospital at ten next morning when the nurse suggested that two of the four visitors should go out for a while. Miss Hunter and her sister withdrew leaving Susan and Gillian with the patient.

"Will you have to stay in bed at 'Deepdene'?" asked Gillian, wondering how the mistress's homecoming would affect herself and Susan.

"No, indeed, Gillian. I'm well on the way to recovery now. I shall have to rest a good deal at first, and cook and Lucy will want to cosset me, I know. But I intend to finish that special job if it's at all possible." She smiled teasingly at the two girls. "You needn't be afraid that you will be chained to my side. You have shown that you are to be trusted, and I intend to go on trusting you."

Miss Francis proved as good as her word. During the week that followed she encouraged the girls to be out of doors whenever it was fine. They went to Rockleigh for riding lessons as usual and received permission to accept an invitation sent via Miss Pamela Hunter, to take tea with Mrs. Perry on her birthday.

When Susan and Gillian arrived at 'Twin Gables' they were surprised to find Mrs. Newton and Robin seated in the parlour. Mrs. Perry introduced them as her niece and great nephew.

"Susan and I have met before," smiled Mrs. Newton, and went on to tell how Susan had frustrated Robin's bid to dash out into the Minchington road.

"He evidently bears you no malice," laughed Mrs. Perry as Robin offered Susan one of his chocolate drops.

They all enjoyed the birthday tea and some games with Robin afterwards, and when Mrs. Newton was leaving she said to the girls, "I'm going to write to your Miss Francis and ask if you can spend a day at Southernwood Farm. Miss Hunter, and Auntie here, will vouch for my respectability."

She kept her promise, too, and after making discreet enquiries Miss Francis allowed the girls to visit the farm. They spent blissful hours among chicks and ducklings, and tiny pink piglets, to say nothing of other fascinating creatures, and watched the cows being milked.

After a good deal of coaxing Mr. Newton even showed them how to drive the tractor, and allowed them to operate the machine which chopped and mixed food for some of the stock. Robin followed the visitors like a shadow, though nothing would induce him to go with the girls to inspect the row of beehives beside a herbaceous border in the farmhouse garden.

"He was stung once," explained his mother, "his own fault, needless to say, but it has given him a wholesome respect for bees."

At tea-time the 'hands' came in from the fields, and the whole company sat down to tea in the big farmhouse kitchen.

"I've heard of groaning boards," whispered Susan to Gillian, "and now I've seen one."

There was a pleasant buzz of talk and laughter while the piles of eatables steadily diminished, and Mrs. Newton replenished cups from an enormous enamel teapot. The farmer and his wife were liked and respected by their work people, and the farm atmosphere was happy in consequence.

Susan and Gillian had been wondering why they had seen no sign of Brian Timms, and when he failed to appear at tea, Sue asked Mrs. Newton the reason.

"He only came to us temporarily," the farmer's wife told her, "and two days ago he left to start work at the stud on the moor. Now everyone has finished eating, so if you want to try your skill at butter-making we had better go to the dairy straight away."

After hilarious but unsuccessful attempts on the part of both Susan and Gillian to make the butter 'come' they said 'goodbye' to their kind hostess, and returned to school to give Miss Francis an enthusiastic account of life as it was lived at Southernwood Farm.

Next morning when the two girls presented themselves at Rockleigh for their riding lesson Miss Hunter informed them rather mysteriously that there would be no jumping that day, as they had an extra long ride in prospect. She refused to say where they were going but led her little cavalcade across country by bridle paths and lanes, until, climbing a short steep slope, they found themselves on the edge of the moor.

Susan and Gillian exchanged puzzled glances, while Miss Julie exclaimed, "What's the big idea, Pam?"

"We're going to visit the stud," smiled her sister. "Colonel Reeves 'phoned last night while you were out, Julie, and invited us all. As Brian Timms' new boss, he wanted to thank me for my recommendations. He thinks Brian will prove to be just the lad he's been wanting."

The four rode on across the moor, Susan and Gillian greatly delighted at the prospect of seeing the stud. Colonel and Mrs. Reeves welcomed them warmly, and carried them off to the house for coffee before they started their tour of inspection. Miss Hunter and her sister were impressed by the efficient way in which the stud was run, Gillian and Susan loved the spirited little ponies, with their soft brown eyes and flowing manes. After a while Colonel Reeves suggested that the two girls might like to ride through the paddocks and watch the grooms schooling some of the ponies, as he had business to discuss with Miss Hunter and her sister.

Susan mounted Puck, and waited in the stableyard for Gillian to join her on Silverspot. She was rather close to one of the loose boxes and suddenly the pony in it stretched his neck over the half door, and gave Puck's flank a nip. It wasn't a really hard bite but, startled, Puck reared, and tore out of the stableyard. Susan was too good a horsewoman to be seriously alarmed, and she felt sure she would be able to rein the frightened pony in before very long. Across the paddocks they flew, and Brian Timms, schooling a pony in the last one, saw them coming. His face paled. He knew, what Sue did not, that beyond the low wall which marked the boundary of the stud on this side was an almost sheer drop into a deep narrow coombe. Puck, used to jumping, would clear the wall like a bird, and down would go pony and rider to serious injury, possibly even death. Brian's feet scarcely seemed to touch the ground as he raced to intercept the pony. For one awful moment he thought he'd missed, then managed to grab the bridle. Talking soothingly, he hung on grimly, and brought quivering, foam-flecked Puck to a halt whilst still several feet from the wall.

"Thank you, Brian," said Sue coolly, "but I could have managed. I should have reined him in soon."

"Perhaps not soon enough," gasped Brian. "Come and look."

Still holding Puck's bridle he advanced to the wall.

"Oh!" cried Susan, peering over. Her blue eyes dilated.

"You probably saved my life, Brian," she added quietly.

Brian reddened, and shrugged disparagingly. "I owed you a good turn, anyway. I thought I owed you a bad one, and that's why I was going to keep your Shepherdess, but I believe now I was wrong."

"Sue! Sue!" called Gillian, as she cantered towards them, "you might have waited for me."

"Sorry, Puck decided otherwise," apologised Susan, "but I haven't watched any schooling yet, so we'll go and watch together."

"I won't tell Jill about my narrow escape," she thought, "until it's a bit less frightening."

Susan still omitted to mention it when the two girls were preparing for bed in the Primrose Room, and talking over their visit to the stud.

"After our grand time this morning, and the lovely day at Southernwood Farm, we can hardly expect anything else," concluded Gillian.

"No," agreed Sue, "we mustn't be greedy. It's jog-trot now for the rest of the holidays. No more red-letter days."

CHAPTER XVII

MISS CASTLETON RETURNS

SUSAN'S prediction that there would be no more red-letter days remained unfulfilled, for the noon post next day brought a note from Mrs. Melsom.

'Dear Susan and Gillian,' she wrote, 'I hope you have not yet made any arrangements for to-morrow, because I should like you to come here to lunch and tea, if Miss Francis will give permission. Two of Dr. Melsom's nieces are to spend the day with us, and you could have some tennis in the afternoon, and after tea we might manage to play the games which were crowded out on your last visit. I think you will like Anita and Lyn, and we will hope for a fine day. Come about half-past twelve.

Yours very sincerely,

Grace Melsom.'

As soon as they had read the letter the girls rushed to tell Miss Francis of the invitation. She readily gave permission for its acceptance, as several hours alone would give her a golden opportunity to catch up on arrears of her special work.

The weather was fine, as Mrs. Melsom had hoped, and Gillian and Susan liked Anita and Lyn straight away. They had several good games of tennis, exchanged school news, and views on nearly every subject under the sun, and by the time they went indoors for the 'celebration tea' were firm friends.

After tea they tried their skill at a number of games,

had some fast and furious quizzes and finished up with 'twenty questions'. Everyone was sorry when Dr. Melsom said, after a startled glance at the clock,

"I must see about driving Anita and Lyn home or they will never be allowed to visit us again."

Miss Francis had promised to call for Susan and Gillian, and they were waiting for her to arrive when Mrs. Melsom left them for a few minutes and returned carrying two tiny square packets. She handed one to each of the girls, smiling at their surprised expressions.

"Just a little memento of the discovery of Uncle Stephen's real birthday present," she told them.

With eager fingers the girls unwrapped the packets and disclosed two marcasite brooches in the form of a toad.

"How lovely!" squealed Gillian, "even a toad looks pretty in marcasite."

"I call him a very handsome fellow," declared Sue stroking her brooch, and in chorus the girls thanked Mrs. Melsom, and assured her they would treasure their toads always.

Four days before school re-opened Miss Castleton returned, sunburned and refreshed, from her holiday in Italy. First, she had to hear full details of Miss Francis's sudden illness, and to satisfy herself that the mistress was really almost well again. Then she must enjoy cook's feast of welcome before unpacking her cases. When she finally adjourned to her sitting-room Gillian and Susan thought it might be a suitable moment to present the substitute Shepherdess.

In an agitated duet they explained how they had broken the Dresden Shepherdess on the first day of the holidays.

"I missed it directly I came into the room," said

Miss Castleton austerely, "and I was just about to ring for Lucy to enquire what had happened."

"We're very sorry," apologised Gillian.

"We've brought you another one," put in Susan nervously, proffering the parcel.

"As you are sorry and have provided a substitute, I suppose I must forgive you," smiled Miss Castleton, softening.

She unfolded the tissue paper which cloaked the Dresden Shepherdess, and as the little figure came to light surveyed it in delighted surprise. It was obviously much better than the one which the girls had broken. She picked the figure up and examined its base.

"The crossed swords mark!" she exclaimed excitedly. "If this is genuine, girls, you've found an old and rare specimen of a Dresden Shepherdess. Mine was only a very ordinary reproduction. May I ask where you bought this one, and how much you paid for it?"

"We bought it from Mrs. Perry at Rocombe, and it cost five pounds," replied Susan rather reluctantly.

Then in response to Miss Castleton's raised eyebrows, and evident expectation of an explanation, Gillian briefly explained how they had earned the money.

Miss Castleton shook her head, though her eyes twinkled.

"I'm glad I did not know what you were doing while I was enjoying my holiday, but fortunately you came to no harm. Now, I have to go to London on business to-morrow, so I will take the Dresden Shepherdess with me, and have it examined in the Ceramics Department of the Victoria and Albert Museum. The experts there will tell me if the crossed swords mark is genuine, and whether the figure is, in fact, an old and rare piece. If it is, I am sure it will be worth a great deal more than five pounds, and Mrs. Perry must be given the opportunity to have it back."

Susan and Gillian exchanged dismayed glances. It would be a 'sell' if that happened after all their trouble.

"Run away now, girls," commanded Miss Castleton, "because I am going to be very busy. I shall see you at prayers this evening, and I will let you know what the experts say about the Dresden Shepherdess."

CHAPTER XVIII

EVERYONE IS SATISFIED

MISS CASTLETON went off to London very early next morning and did not return until long after Susan and Gillian were in bed. The two girls begged for permission to stay up, but Miss Francis was firm in her refusal.

"Miss Castleton will be much too tired to bother with you to-night," she told them. "Make up your minds to go to sleep straight away and the morning will soon be here. Miss Castleton won't keep you long in suspense then, I'm sure."

Miss Francis proved to be right. Just as Susan and Gillian were going out into the garden after breakfast next morning Miss Castleton came downstairs and beckoned them into her sitting-room.

"I know you are anxious to hear what happened," she smiled. "The museum experts confirmed that the crossed swords mark is quite genuine. So for five pounds you've managed to buy an old and rare specimen of a Dresden Shepherdess. Of course, the museum people did not value the figure; they never will, but I shall get it valued without delay. When I am in Duncombe this morning I shall take it in to Mr. Wade, the antique dealer, who is an authority on china, and ask him what it is worth."

At lunch time Miss Castleton joined Miss Francis and the two girls in the Junior Common Room looking flushed and excited.

"Mr. Wade offered to buy the Shepherdess from me

for a hundred pounds, cash down," she smiled, "but I had to tell him it was not for sale. We must give Mrs. Perry the opportunity to buy it back for five pounds, though I'm hoping, very much hoping, that she will allow me to pay her another ninety-five pounds and keep it for my own. I should love to possess a rare and beautiful piece such as this, though you may be sure," eyeing the girls severely, "that if Mrs. Perry allows me to buy it I shall not place it on the bureau to be a target for flying parcels; I shall put it away carefully until I retire."

The conversation switched to other matters during the rest of the meal, but when they rose from the table Miss Castleton turned to Susan and Gillian with a proposition.

"If you have not made any plans for this afternoon, perhaps you will take a note to Mrs. Perry for me. She is not on the telephone and I should like to know whether I am to be allowed to keep the Shepherdess. You can stay to tea if you are invited, but you must catch the six o'clock bus back."

The two girls welcomed a chance to visit Mrs. Perry and Rufus, and were soon setting off gaily with Miss Castleton's note. But they sat rather anxiously in the kitchen of 'Twin Gables' watching Mrs. Perry read it, and wondered what would happen. Incredulity and delight were mirrored in her face, and they waited to see whether she would decide to buy back her treasure.

"Well!" she exclaimed, "to think my little Shepherdess is worth a hundred pounds. No wonder Granny told me to take care of it."

"Do you want to buy the Shepherdess back again?" asked Gillian breathlessly.

Mrs. Perry shook her head. "No. I know Miss

Castleton would like to keep her, and a hundred pounds will be a most wonderful windfall to me just now. It seems too good to be true. You must stay to tea and talk about it. Fortunately, I baked this morning, and made some of those little cakes you liked so much on my birthday."

As soon as first cups of tea had been passed she exclaimed again: "This hundred pound surprise seems too good to be true. The repairs to the roof are going to cost much more than the original estimate, and I've been so worried. Now, I can not only pay the bill, but I can visit Sylvia. I shall leave the workmen in possession of 'Twin Gables' and stay with Sylvia until they're finished."

"What about Rufus?" Susan looked up from giving him a piece of cake.

"Rufus will stay here," said his mistress decidedly. "The builder is one of his friends, and he'll feed him and take him for walks. Rufus won't mind staying. He will have company during the day, and can guard the house at night. The old fellow doesn't like travelling and strange places, and he would be terribly jealous of the fuss I shall make of my baby grandson."

Mrs. Perry was thrilled by the prospect of a holiday, and overjoyed at the thought of seeing her daughter so soon, and so unexpectedly.

After tea she brought out an album of snapshots to show the two girls, and they had the greatest difficulty in tearing themselves away in time to catch the six o'clock bus.

"We simply dare not miss it, Mrs. Perry," dimpled Susan. "If we do, not even the news that she can keep the Shepherdess will save us from Miss Castleton's wrath."

"Tell her I'm pleased for her to have it," smiled Mrs. Perry, as she and Rufus saw them off.

"Miss Castleton will be pleased she *can* have it, and we're pleased we didn't have to let it go, so everybody is pleased," quipped Gillian.

She and Susan walked along the lane talking in comradely fashion. Their friendship had deepened during the weeks of holiday, and had been cemented by shared experiences. Since Susan had kept her resolution to ask Gillian about her talk with Miss Blain, the two girls had enjoyed several talks together. Now they shared the greatest experience of all, for Susan, too, was one of the sheep who hear the Saviour's voice and love Him and follow Him.

Gillian glanced at her watch as they turned along the village street, and they broke into a run. The bus was about to start, the conductor actually had his hand on the bell, but seeing the girls running he kindly waited for them. When they had regained their breath, and while the bus cruised along the lanes towards Duncombe, they discussed the highlights of the holidays.

"To-morrow will be the last day on our own," sighed Susan. "The day after, everyone will be back, and we shall begin another term."

"But these holidays have been fun, haven't they? And to think how miserable I felt when I saw the coach disappearing down the drive that first day," exclaimed Gillian. "We have had fun," she repeated, "and it's rather strange when you come to think of it that quite a number of things would never have happened if I hadn't broken Miss Castleton's Dresden Shepherdess."

"If I hadn't missed catching my parcel," corrected Susan, and her dimples were once more in evidence.